on this day

on this day

Over 1,800 Arsenal facts, games, goals, transfers and trivia

Leigh Edwards

hamlyn

First published in Great Britain
in 2006 by Hamlyn, a division of
Octopus Publishing Group Ltd,
2–4 Heron Quays, London E14 4JP

ISBN-13: 978-0-600-61030-4
ISBN-10: 0-600-61030-6

A CIP catalogue record for this book is
available from the British Library

Printed and bound in the UK

10 9 8 7 6 5 4 3 2 1

**All statistics correct up to the
end of the 2005/06 season.**

contents

Introduction

On 7th May 2006, Arsenal played their last game at Highbury. It was yet another key date in the story of a club with an amazing history.

Over 1,800 key facts are detailed in this fascinating reference book. It is a progression of the popular 'On This Day' series that appeared in Arsenal's programme throughout the historic 2005/06 campaign.

Five significant events have been selected from Arsenal's history, as well as from the football world as a whole, for each day of the year, including memorable matches, notable transfers and managerial changes. During the months of the football season, August to May, there are so many events and stories that selecting which to include

is no easy task, whereas during the summer months the emphasis inevitably switches to players' birthdays, transfer activity and Arsenal stars appearing in international tournaments.

You will be able to 'dip in' and remind yourself of key moments from legendary games, such as the title-winning game at Anfield in 1989, the amazing 5–1 victory over Inter Milan at the San Siro in 2006 or the feats of Bertie Mee's Double winning side in 1971. More sombre occasions, such as the premature death of Herbert Chapman in 1934 are recalled, as well as significant feats such as the first FA Cup win in 1930 and Thierry Henry becoming the Club's all-time scorer.

On This Day will provide you with a reference for pre-match discussions and post-match analysis, and will recall some great memories. Happy reading...

1 January

1923   Leading marksman Bobby Turnbull scored four times in Arsenal's rousing 5–0 First Division victory over Blackburn Rovers at Ewood Park.

1937   Arsenal swept to a 5–0 First Division win against Bolton Wanderers at Burnden Park with four goals by Ted Drake plus another from Jackie Milne.

1990   England international Alan Smith netted twice in the Gunners' 4–1 First Division victory over Crystal Palace at Highbury.

2003   Arsenal's 3–2 Premiership win over Chelsea produced four late goals, including strikes by Giovanni van Bronckhorst and Thierry Henry.

2005   Two goals by Freddie Ljungberg plus another from Robin van Persie gave the Gunners a 3–1 Premiership win at Charlton Athletic.

2 January

1915   Harry King scored four goals in Arsenal's crushing 5–1 Second Division victory over Wolverhampton Wanderers at Highbury.

1960   Dennis Evans, Joe Haverty, Mel Charles and Len Wills scored in the Gunners' thrilling 4–4 First Division draw against Wolverhampton Wanderers.

1971   The Ibrox Stadium disaster left 66 dead after Glasgow Rangers' late equalizer against Celtic led to crush barriers giving way.

1989   Arsenal led the First Division after goals by Paul Merson and Michael Thomas secured a 2–0 win at home to Tottenham Hotspur.

1993   Leading marksman Ian Wright grabbed a hat-trick in Arsenal's 3–1 FA Cup third-round win over Yeovil Town at Huish Park.

3 January

1903 Billy Gooing, Walter Anderson and Billy Linward scored in the Gunners' 3–1 Second Division win at home to Preston North End.

1948 Two goals by Ronnie Rooke plus another from Reg Lewis gave title-chasing Arsenal a 3–2 First Division win at home over Sheffield United.

1951 Left-back Dennis Evans joined Arsenal from non-League Ellesmere Port. He scored 12 times in 207 games for the Gunners between 1953/54 and 1959/60.

1959 Arsenal gained a 3–2 First Division win at Leicester City with two goals by Len Julians plus another from Jimmy Bloomfield.

2000 Emmanuel Petit's first-half strike gave Arsène Wenger's side a 1–1 Premiership draw at bottom-of-the-table Sheffield Wednesday.

4 January

1896 David Howat played his last game for the Gunners as Henry Boyd scored twice in the 5–0 Second Division drubbing of Midlands club Loughborough Town, who left the League in 1900.

1947 Ronnie Rooke and Reg Lewis netted two goals apiece in the Gunners' 4–1 First Division win over Sunderland at Roker Park.

1975 Mick Mahon's goal gave non-League giant-killers Wimbledon a shock 1–0 FA Cup third-round victory at top-flight Burnley.

1986 Charlie Nicholas' hat-trick plus a goal by Graham Rix gave Arsenal a 4–3 FA Cup third-round victory at Grimsby Town.

2003 Dennis Bergkamp scored his 100th goal for Arsenal in the 2–0 FA Cup third-round victory at home to Oxford United.

5 January

1935   Ted Drake and Eddie Hapgood scored as title-chasing Arsenal gained a 2–0 First Division victory over Liverpool at Anfield.

1957   Two goals by David Herd plus others from Derek Tapscott and Joe Haverty earned a 4–2 FA Cup third-round win over Stoke City.

1958   Central defender Steve Walford was born in Highgate, London. He netted three goals in 77 First Division games for the Gunners during 1977/78.

1991   Strikes by Alan Smith and Anders Limpar gave George Graham's side a 2–1 FA Cup third-round triumph over Sunderland at Highbury.

2002   Thierry Henry, Freddie Ljungberg, Kanu and Dennis Bergkamp scored in Arsenal's 4–2 FA Cup third-round victory over Watford at Vicarage Road.

6 January

1934   Legendary manager Herbert Chapman, 55, died in London from pneumonia. He masterminded Arsenal's first League championship successes, in 1930/31, 1932/33, 1933/34 and 1934/35, and the Gunners' initial FA Cup triumph in 1930.

1938   England international winger Joe Hulme was sold to Huddersfield Town. He netted 107 goals in 333 games for Arsenal.

1970   Scotland Under-23 winger Peter Marinello joned Arsenal from Hibernian. He scored five times in 51 outings between 1969/70 and 1972/73.

1973   Strikes by Ray Kennedy, George Armstrong and Alan Ball gave Arsenal a 3–1 First Division victory at home to Manchester United.

1998   Ian Wright and Marc Overmars scored to give the Gunners a 2–1 Coca-Cola Cup fifth-round win over West Ham United at Upton Park.

7 January

1978   Malcolm Macdonald and Frank Stapleton netted two goals each in Arsenal's stirring 5–0 FA Cup third-round victory at Sheffield United.

1984   AFC Bournemouth beat holders Manchester United 2–0 in the FA Cup third round with goals by Milton Graham and Ian Thompson.

1988   Scotland international striker Charlie Nicholas joined Aberdeen. He scored 54 times in 184 outings for Arsenal between 1983/84 and 1987/88. Later he returned to Celtic, then ended his playing days with Clyde.

1989   Goals by Tony Rains and Matthew Hanlan gave non-League Sutton United a 2–1 FA Cup third-round win over top-flight Coventry City.

2004   Kanu's first-half strike gave Arsène Wenger's title-chasing Gunners a 1–1 Premiership draw against Everton at Goodison Park.

8 January

1887   Non-League Erith were beaten 6-1 in a friendly at Plumstead Common in Royal Arsenal's first fixture after the name was changed from Dial Square.

1898   Fergus Hunt, John Anderson, Billy White, Jimmy Brock and David Hannah all scored in a 5–1 Second Division win over Newton Heath, who later became Manchester United.

1949   Goals from Ian McPherson, Don Roper and Doug Lishman gave Arsenal a 3–0 FA Cup third-round win over Tottenham Hotspur.

1957   England B international forward Don Roper rejoined Southampton. He netted 88 goals in 297 First Division outings while at Highbury.

1989   Paul Merson scored twice to give George Graham's side a 2–2 FA Cup third-round draw against West Ham United at Upton Park.

9 January

1932   Cliff Bastin scored four goals and David Jack a hat-trick in Arsenal's record 11–1 FA Cup third-round win at home to Lancashire club Darwen.

1954   Don Roper netted twice as Tom Whittaker's team gained a convincing 5–1 FA Cup third-round victory over Aston Villa at Highbury.

1961   Football players, led by PFA chairman Jimmy Hill, celebrated as the maximum wage of £20 a week was abolished.

1979   Charlton Athletic's Mike Flanagan and Derek Hales were sent off for fighting each other during the FA Cup tie against Maidstone United.

2005   Arsenal recovered from going a goal down to win 2–1 at home to Stoke City in the FA Cup third round with goals from Jose Antonio Reyes and Robin van Persie.

10 January

1920   Jock Rutherford, Fred Groves, Alex Graham and Fred Pagnam scored in a 4–2 FA Cup first-round win over Rochdale at Highbury.

1948   Billy Elliott's strike gave Bradford Park Avenue a shock 1–0 FA Cup third-round victory at First Division leaders Arsenal.

1953   Doug Lishman, Cliff Holton, Jimmy Logie and Don Roper netted in Arsenal's 4–0 FA Cup third-round win over Doncaster Rovers.

1996   David Ginola was sent off as Ian Wright's double gave Arsenal a 2–0 Coca Cola Cup fifth-round win at home to Newcastle United.

2004   Robert Pires and Freddie Ljungberg scored in the second half as the Gunners gained a 4–1 Premiership win over Middlesbrough.

11 January

1936   Cliff Bastin and Ted Drake netted two goals apiece in Arsenal's comfortable 5–1 FA Cup third-round victory at Bristol Rovers.

1951   Reg Lewis scored twice as Arsenal defeated Carlisle United 4–1 in an FA Cup third-round replay at Brunton Park.

1975   Bertie Mee's side gained a 2–1 First Division win at home to Carlisle United with goals from John Radford and Alex Cropley.

1979   Midfielder Brian Talbot joined Arsenal from Ipswich Town. He scored 49 times in 326 games for the Gunners between 1978/79 and 1984/85.

1997   Dennis Bergkamp was sent off and Tony Adams' own goal gave Sunderland a 1–0 Premiership win at home to the Gunners.

12 January

1928   Belfast-born international left back Andy Kennedy moved to Everton. He made 122 First Division appearances while at Highbury.

1952   Leading marksman Doug Lishman scored twice in Arsenal's 5–0 FA Cup third-round victory over Norwich City at Carrow Road.

1956   Non-League Bedford Town were seconds away from beating Arsenal in an FA Cup third-round replay when the Gunners equalized, then snatched victory in extra time.

1993   Ian Wright scored twice in his last game before suspension as Arsenal beat Nottingham Forest 2–0 in the Coca-Cola Cup fifth round.

2003   Thierry Henry scored twice, including his 100th goal for Arsenal, in the 4–0 Premiership win over Birmingham City at St Andrews.

13 January

1945   Defender Peter Simpson was born in Gorleston, Norfolk. He featured in Arsenal's 1970/71 Double triumph and scored 15 goals in 477 games between 1963/64 and 1977/78.

1970   Arsenal defeated French side Rouen 1–0 at Highbury in the second leg of the European Fairs Cup third-round tie with a goal from Jon Sammels.

1979   Brian Talbot made his debut as goals by David Price and Frank Stapleton gave Arsenal a 2–1 First Division win over Nottingham Forest.

1995   Welsh international striker John Hartson was signed from Luton Town. He netted 14 goals in 53 Premiership games for Arsenal before joining West Ham United.

1996   Strikes by Paul Merson, David Platt and Glenn Helder gave the Gunners a 3–2 Premiership victory at Middlesbrough.

14 January

1899   David Hannah scored twice as the Gunners stormed to a 6–0 Second Division victory over Lancashire club Darwen at the Manor Ground.

1961   David Herd grabbed a hat-trick as George Swindin's side gained a thrilling 5–4 First Division victory over Manchester City.

1998   Double-chasing Arsenal triumphed 4–3 on penalties after being held to a 1–1 draw at Port Vale in the FA Cup third-round replay.

1999   Notts County's 15-year-old starlet Jermaine Pennant moved to Highbury. He netted three goals in 12 Premiership games for Arsenal.

2006   Thierry Henry equalled Cliff Bastin's record of 150 League goals with a hat-trick in Arsenal's 7–0 Premiership thrashing of Middlesbrough.

15 January

1949   Jimmy Logie scored twice as Tom Whittaker's team secured an exciting 5–3 First Division win at home to Sheffield United.

1969   Arsenal striker John Radford won the first of his two full England caps in the 1–1 draw against Romania at Wembley.

1972   Goals from George Armstrong and Alan Ball gave holders Arsenal a 2–0 FA Cup third-round victory at Swindon Town.

1983   Graham Rix, Vladimir Petrovic and John Hollins scored in the Gunners' 3–0 First Division win over Stoke City at Highbury.

2000   Thierry Henry and Davor Suker netted two goals apiece as Arsenal gained a 4–1 Premiership victory at home to Sunderland.

16 January

1920   Welsh international full back Walley Barnes, capped 22 times, was born in Brecon. He netted 11 goals in 267 First Division games for Arsenal between 1946/47 and 1955/56.

1926   Two goals by Jimmy Brain plus another from Charlie Buchan gave Arsenal a 3–2 First Division win over Manchester United.

1937   Ted Drake and Alf Kirchen contributed two goals each as the Gunners eased to a 5–1 win at Chesterfield in the FA Cup third round.

1957   Scotland Under-21 midfielder Trevor Ross was born in Ashton-under-Lyne, Lancashire. He scored nine times in 67 outings while at Highbury from 1974/75 to 1977/78.

1999   New Nottingham Forest manager Ron Atkinson saw Martin Keown's strike clinch Arsenal's 1–0 Premiership win at the City Ground.

17 January

1903   Tommy Shanks scored twice as Harry Bradshaw's team secured a 4–0 Second Division win over Barnsley at the Manor Ground.

1932   Scotland international forward Jackie Henderson, who earned seven caps, was born in Glasgow. He netted 29 goals in 111 games for Arsenal between 1958/59 and 1961/62.

1948   Reg Lewis scored in Arsenal's 1–1 First Division draw away to title rivals Manchester United, watched by a record 83,260 crowd.

1953   Doug Lishman bagged two goals as championship-chasing Arsenal gained a 5–3 First Division triumph at home to Wolverhampton Wanderers.

1968   George Graham, John Radford and Bob McNab scored in Arsenal's 3–2 League Cup semi-final first-leg win over Huddersfield Town (see 6 February, page 26, for second leg).

18 January

1930   Herbert Chapman's side secured a 2–2 First Division draw at Burnley with goals from Cliff Bastin and David Jack.

1975   Central defender Jeff Blockley was sold to Leicester City. He scored once in 62 matches during his Highbury career which began in 1972.

1977   Malcolm Macdonald and Trevor Francis both scored hat-tricks in Arsenal's 3–3 First Division draw at Birmingham City.

1983   Tony Woodcock's second-half strike gave the Gunners a 1–0 Milk Cup fifth-round win at home to Sheffield Wednesday.

2004   Arsenal rose to the top of the Premiership after Thierry Henry scored twice to clinch a 2–0 victory at Aston Villa.

19 January

1898   Scotland international goalkeeper Bill Harper was born in Tarbrax, Lanarkshire. Before becoming a professional footballer he worked as a blacksmith.

1929   Leading marksman David Jack scored twice in Arsenal's 4–0 First Division victory over Portsmouth at Highbury.

1977   Cameroon international defender Lauren was born in Lodhji Kribi. He starred in the Gunners' 2001/02 Double success.

2000   Substitute keeper Peggy Arphexad saved penalties from Lee Dixon and Gilles Grimandi as Leicester City beat Arsenal 6–5 on penalties in the FA Cup fourth-round replay.

2003   Thierry Henry netted a hat-trick, including his first headed goal in the Premiership, as Arsenal won 3–1 at home to West Ham United.

20 January

1951   Reg Lewis scored twice to give Tom Whittaker's side a 2–2 First Division draw against Huddersfield Town at Leeds Road.

1959   Winger Alan Skirton joined Arsenal from non-League Bath City. He netted 54 goals in 154 appearances during his sojourn at Highbury before leaving to join Blackpool in 1966. He went on to become commercial manager at Yeovil Town.

1988   Nigel Winterburn's second-half strike secured the Gunners a 1–0 Littlewoods Cup fifth-round victory at Sheffield Wednesday.

1994   Former Manchester United manager Sir Matt Busby, who led the team to their 1968 European Cup Final triumph, died aged 84.

2006   Arsène Wenger signed Theo Walcott from Southampton after the 16-year-old starlet had impressed for Saints in the Championship.

21 January

1911   Arsenal were leading Aston Villa 2–1 at the Manor Ground when the First Division match was abandoned in the 80th minute due to bad light.

1925   Scotland international wing-half Alex Forbes, who was capped 14 times, was born in Dundee. He scored 20 times in 217 First Division games for the Gunners between 1947/48 and 1955/56.

1933   Cliff Bastin scored twice as title-chasing Arsenal gained a 2–1 First Division win over Manchester City at Highbury.

1987   Arsenal beat Nottingham Forest 2–0 at home in the Littlewoods Cup fifth round with goals by Charlie Nicholas and Martin Hayes.

1995   John Hartson scored his first goal for the Gunners to clinch a 1–0 Premiership victory over Coventry City at Highfield Road.

22 January

1921   Two goals by Jock Rutherford plus another from Bert White earned Arsenal a 3–2 First Division win at home to Tottenham Hotspur.

1927   Charlie Buchan's goal gave Arsenal a 1–1 First Division draw with Sheffield United, in the first match broadcast live by BBC radio.

1979   Arsenal finally beat Sheffield Wednesday 2–0 in the FA Cup third-round fourth replay at Leicester with goals by Steve Gatting and Frank Stapleton.

1985   Paul Mariner and Brian Talbot netted two goals apiece in Arsenal's 7–2 FA Cup third-round replay romp at home against Hereford United.

1994   Ian Wright's first-half penalty earned the Gunners a 1–1 Premiership draw against struggling Oldham Athletic at Highbury.

23 January

1932   Jack Lambert scored twice as Herbert Chapman's side defeated Plymouth Argyle 4–2 in an FA Cup fourth-round encounter at Highbury.

1937   Goals by Cliff Bastin, Ted Drake and Ray Bowden gave Arsenal a 3–0 First Division victory over Wolverhampton Wanderers.

1965   Leading marksman Joe Baker netted two goals in the Gunners' nerve-tingling 4–3 First Division triumph over Leicester City at Highbury.

2002   Strikes by Giovanni van Bronckhorst, Thierry Henry and Sylvain Wiltord secured Arsenal's 3–1 Premiership win at Leicester City.

2003   England Under-21 central defender Matthew Upson joined Birmingham City. The young central defender made 39 appearances for the Gunners after joining the Club from Luton in 1997.

24 January

1959   Vic Groves scored twice to save the blushes of George Swindin's side in a 2–2 FA Cup fourth-round draw at Colchester United.

1978   Liam Brady's disputed penalty saw Arsenal through to a 1–0 League Cup fifth-round replay win at home to Manchester City.

1999   Marc Overmars and Dennis Bergkamp netted in the Gunners' 2–1 FA Cup fourth-round victory at Wolverhampton Wanderers.

2000   Freddie Ljungberg found the net as Arsenal, playing their seventh match in 22 days, gained a 1–1 Premiership draw at Manchester United.

2004   Two goals by Freddie Ljungberg and one each by Dennis Bergkamp and David Bentley gave Arsène Wenger's team a comprehensive 4–1 FA Cup fourth-round win over Middlesbrough at Highbury.

25 January

1936   George Allison's side drew 2–2 at Liverpool in the FA Cup fourth round with goals from Ray Bowden and Joe Hulme.

1964   Johnny MacLeod, George Armstrong and Joe Baker scored in Arsenal's 3–3 FA Cup fourth-round draw at West Bromwich Albion.

1986   Ian Allinson netted twice as the Gunners trounced Rotherham United 5–1 at Highbury in the FA Cup fourth round.

1993   Arsenal fought back with goals by Ray Parlour and Paul Merson to draw 2–2 at home to Leeds United in the FA Cup fourth round.

2003   Francis Jeffers scored twice on his 22nd birthday in Arsenal's 5–1 FA Cup fourth-round victory over Nationwide Conference team Farnborough Town at Highbury.

26 January

1901   Two goals by Ralph Gaudie plus another from Alex Main enabled the Gunners to draw 3–3 in their away Second Division encounter with Lincoln City.

1957   Jack Crayston's side won 2–0 at Newport County in the FA Cup fourth round with goals by Derek Tapscott and David Herd.

1963   As the 'Big Freeze' continued to cause widespread fixture postponements, the Pools Panel forecast results for the first time.

1980   Sammy Nelson and Brian Talbot registered to give holders Arsenal a 2–0 FA Cup fourth-round win at home to Brighton and Hove Albion.

1985   In one of the biggest giant-killing acts of modern times, Keith Houchen's last-minute penalty gave York City FA Cup fourth-round victory over Arsenal at Bootham Crescent.

27 January

1934 Jimmy Dunne, Cliff Bastin and Pat Beasley scored two goals each in a 7–0 FA Cup fourth-round win at home to Crystal Palace.

1951 Two goals by Reg Lewis plus another from Don Roper enabled Arsenal to prevail 3–2 at home to Northampton Town in the fourth round of the FA Cup.

1997 Central defender Andy Linighan was sold to Crystal Palace. He netted eight goals in 155 games for Arsenal and headed the winner against Sheffield Wednesday in the 1993 FA Cup Final replay.

2001 Sylvain Wiltord netted twice as Arsène Wenger's side pulverized QPR 6–0 at Loftus Road in the FA Cup fourth round.

2002 Martin Keown and Dennis Bergkamp were sent off after the Dutchman had scored in Arsenal's 1–0 FA Cup fourth-round victory over Liverpool.

28 January

1928 Joe Hulme was on target twice as Herbert Chapman's team prevailed by the odd goal in seven in an FA Cup fourth-round thriller at Highbury.

1931 David Jack netted four goals and Jack Lambert plundered a hat-trick in Arsenal's 9–1 First Division annihilation of Grimsby Town at Highbury – the Gunners' biggest ever First Division win.

1959 David Herd scored twice as the Gunners triumphed 4–0 at home to Colchester United in an FA Cup fourth-round replay.

1978 Strikes by Alan Sunderland and Malcolm Macdonald clinched a 2–1 FA Cup fourth-round win over Wolverhampton Wanderers.

1998 Arsenal defeated Chelsea 2–1 in the Coca-Cola Cup semi-final first leg with goals from Marc Overmars and Stephen Hughes. Chelsea won the second leg 3–1.

29 January

1906   Goalkeeper Hugh McDonald joined Arsenal from the Ayrshire club Beith. He made 94 League appearances during three spells with the Gunners.

1949   Goals by player-boss Alec Stock and Eric Bryant gave non-League Yeovil Town a 2–1 FA Cup fourth-round win over Sunderland.

1972   Charlie George scored twice as the Gunners stormed to a 5–0 First Division win over Sheffield United at Bramall Lane.

1988   Right back Lee Dixon joined Arsenal from Stoke City. He netted 28 goals in 614 games as a Gunner between 1987/88 and 2001/02 and is 4th in the Club's highest appearance record.

2003   Goals from Robert Pires and Dennis Bergkamp secured table-topping Arsenal a 2–2 Premiership draw against Liverpool at Anfield.

30 January

1932   Ray Parkin's hat-trick plus a goal by Alex James gave the Gunners a 4–0 First Division victory at home to Manchester City.

1937   Leading marksman Ted Drake scored as Arsenal hammered Manchester United 5–0 at Highbury in the FA Cup fourth round.

1954   Arsenal, despite scoring a second-minute penalty, lost 2–1 at home to giant-killers Norwich City in the FA Cup fourth round.

1987   England Under-21 central defender Tommy Caton joined Oxford United. He scored three times in 95 games during his Arsenal career, which began in 1983 following a transfer from Manchester City.

2004   Spanish international striker Jose Antonio Reyes arrived from Sevilla. He helped Arsenal clinch the Premiership title at the season's end.

31 January

1948   Reg Lewis scored twice as title-hunting Arsenal gained a 3–0 First Division victory over Preston North End at Highbury.

1953   Top scorer Doug Lishman netted as Tom Whittaker's side trounced Bury 6–2 at Highbury in the FA Cup fourth round.

1959   Two goals by Jackie Henderson plus others from Vic Groves and David Herd secured a 4–1 First Division win at Tottenham Hotspur.

1987   Viv Anderson was on the scoresheet twice as the Gunners swept to a 6–1 FA Cup fourth-round victory at home to Plymouth Argyle.

1998   Strikes by Dennis Bergkamp, Tony Adams and Nicolas Anelka gave Arsenal a 3–0 Premiership win over Southampton at Highbury.

1 February

1935   Inside forward Bobby Davidson joined Arsenal from St Johnstone. He scored 13 times in 57 games for the Gunners.

1947   Ronnie Rooke grabbed a hat-trick as George Allison's side rampaged to a 6–2 First Division victory at home to Manchester United.

1956   Centre forward Tommy Lawton joined Kettering Town as player-manager. The legendary England marksman netted 13 goals in 35 outings during a brief Highbury tenure.

1958   Manchester United held on to secure a 5–4 First Division victory in a pulsating contest at Highbury, their last League game before the Munich air disaster.

2003   Two goals by Robert Pires, including a last-minute winner, afforded leaders Arsenal a 2–1 Premiership win at home to Fulham.

2 February

1935   Alex James scored the only hat-trick of his distinguished career in Arsenal's 4–1 First Division victory over Sheffield Wednesday.

1952   Reg Lewis' hat-trick plus a goal by Doug Lishman gave Arsenal a comfortable 4–0 FA Cup fourth-round win over Barnsley at Highbury.

1957   David Herd scored a hat-trick as Jack Crayston's team racked up a 6–3 First Division victory at home to Sheffield Wednesday.

1968   Striker Bobby Gould joined Arsenal from Coventry City. He netted 16 goals in 65 First Division games for the Gunners.

2002   Title contenders Arsenal dropped two points at home to Southampton, with Sylvain Wiltord netting in a 1–1 draw.

3 February

1899   Welsh international left half Bob John was born in Barry Dock. He scored 12 times in 421 League outings for the Gunners, then hung up his boots in 1938.

1942   Scottish Schoolboy defender John Snedden was born in Bonnybridge. He made 83 First Division appearances for the Gunners before moving to Charlton Athletic in 1965.

1973   Alan Ball and Charlie George scored to give Bertie Mee's side a 2–0 FA Cup fourth-round win at home to Bradford City.

1993   Two goals by Ian Wright plus another from Alan Smith secured Arsenal a 3–2 FA Cup fourth-round replay victory at Leeds United.

2001   Dennis Bergkamp's late strike clinched the Gunners' 1–0 Premiership victory over Coventry City at Highfield Road.

4 February

1922   Goals from Reg Boreham and Joe Toner assured Arsenal of a 2–1 First Division victory over Newcastle United at Highbury.

1956   Two strikes by David Herd plus another from Jimmy Bloomfield gave the Gunners a 3–1 First Division win over Sunderland.

1961   Tommy Docherty made his last appearance before leaving Arsenal to coach Chelsea as Geoff Strong scored twice in the 3–3 First Division draw at Newcastle United.

1970   England Under-21 striker Kevin Campbell was born in Lambeth. He scored 59 times in 226 outings as a Gunner between 1987/88 and 1994/95.

1993   England international central defender Martin Keown rejoined the Gunners from Everton, having left Highbury seven years earlier.

5 February

1926   England international winger Joe Hulme joined Arsenal from Blackburn Rovers. As well as being a pacy flankman, he played first-class cricket for Middlesex and later managed Tottenham Hotspur.

1953   Non-League giant-killers Walthamstow Avenue lost 5–2 to Manchester United in an FA Cup fourth-round replay staged at Highbury.

1960   England international winger Brian Marwood was born in Seaham, County Durham. He scored 17 times in 60 outings while at Highbury.

1972   Ronnie Radford and Ricky George scored to give non-League Hereford United a 2–1 FA Cup third-round replay win over Newcastle United.

2005   Thierry Henry broke Ian Wright's record of League goals for the club with his strike in Arsenal's 3–1 Premiership win at Aston Villa.

6 February

1915   Goals from Jock Rutherford and Frank Bradshaw furnished the Gunners with a 2–0 Second Division victory over Leeds City at Highbury.

1932   Herbert Chapman's side notched a 3–1 First Division win at Everton with goals from Cliff Bastin, Joe Hulme and Bob John.

1958   The Munich Air disaster devastated Manchester United's 'Busby Babes' as eight of the legendary young players were killed.

1968   Jon Sammels, David Jenkins and Frank McLintock scored in the 3–1 League Cup semi-final second-leg win at Huddersfield Town (see 2 March, page 38, for final).

1999   Dennis Bergkamp, Marc Overmars, Nicolas Anelka and Ray Parlour were all on target as Arsenal cruised to a 4–0 Premiership triumph at West Ham United's Upton Park.

7 February

1951   Scotland Under-23 midfielder Eddie Kelly was born in Glasgow. He netted 19 goals in 222 outings during his Highbury career from 1969/70 to 1975/76.

1953   Cliff Holton scored twice as Tom Whittaker's team romped to a 4–0 First Division victory at home to Tottenham Hotspur.

1988   Trevor Steven missed a penalty and Perry Groves' early strike clinched a 1–0 Littlewoods Cup semi-final first-leg win at Everton.

1993   Two goals by Alan Smith and Ian Wright's penalty saw Arsenal through to a 3–1 Coca-Cola Cup semi-final first-leg victory at Crystal Palace (see 10 March, page 42).

2004   Arsenal extended their unbeaten Premiership run to a club-record 24 matches with a 3–1 win at Wolverhampton Wanderers.

8 February

1902   Inside left Tom Fitchie scored twice on his debut in the Gunners' emphatic 5–0 Second Division triumph at home to Lincolnshire club Gainsborough Trinity.

1930   Jack Lambert netted a hat-trick as Herbert Chapman's team compiled a 4–0 First Division victory over Everton at Highbury.

1941   Leslie Compton scored a remarkable ten goals in Arsenal's 15–2 London War Cup victory at home to fellow Londoners Clapton Orient, who were later renamed Leyton Orient.

1964   Arsenal gained a 3–2 First Division win at home to Burnley with goals by Geoff Strong, George Armstrong and Terry Anderson.

1998   Two first-half strikes from Stephen Hughes gave the Gunners a 2–0 Premiership victory over Chelsea at Highbury.

9 February

1901   Strikes by Jimmy Tennant and Tommy Low earned Arsenal a 2–0 FA Cup first-round win at home to Blackburn Rovers.

1952   Don Roper and Alex Forbes scored to give the Gunners a 2–1 First Division victory over local rivals Tottenham Hotspur at White Hart Lane.

1979   England international Trevor Francis became Britain's first £1 million player, moving from Birmingham City to Nottingham Forest.

1984   England international striker Paul Mariner, who won 35 caps, arrived from Ipswich Town. He scored 17 times in 70 games for Arsenal before joining Portsmouth in 1986.

2003   Laurent Robert scored and was sent-off as Thierry Henry's goal gave leaders Arsenal a 1–1 Premiership draw at Newcastle United.

10 February

1912 John Flanagan, Alf Common and Charlie Lewis scored in the Gunners' 3–0 First Division win at home to Bolton Wanderers.

1948 Once-capped England international goalkeeper Jimmy Rimmer was born in Southport, Lancashire. He made 146 appearances for the Gunners between 1973/74 and 1976/77.

1951 The Port of Manchester, trying to clear a backlog of ships, banned the workers from attending Manchester United's match with Arsenal.

1999 Arsenal supplied seven players – four English and three French – as World Cup holders France defeated England 2–0 at Wembley.

2002 Arsenal began their Club-record sequence of 14 consecutive wins as Sylvain Wiltord's goal defeated Everton 1–0 at Goodison Park.

11 February

1888 Royal Arsenal drew 3–3 in a friendly against Millwall Rovers in the first match played at the Manor Ground in Plumstead.

1950 Arsenal gained a 2–0 FA Cup fifth-round victory at home to Burnley with goals from Reg Lewis and Denis Compton.

1980 It was announced in a press conference that England international Kevin Keegan would be joining Southampton from SV Hamburg.

1989 Title challengers Arsenal recovered with goals from Paul Merson and Alan Smith to gain a 2–1 First Division win at Millwall.

1995 Ian Selley broke a leg as under-fire boss George Graham saw Arsenal held to a 1–1 Premiership draw by struggling Leicester City at Highbury.

12 February

1898   Fergus Hunt and David Hannah netted two goals apiece as the Gunners cruised to a 4–1 Second Division win at Grimsby Town.

1910   Arsenal wing-half Andy Ducat made his England international debut in the 1–1 draw against Ireland in Belfast.

1927   Charlie Buchan scored to give Herbert Chapman's team a 1–0 First Division victory over Leeds United at Highbury.

1937   Full back Laurie Scott joined Arsenal from Bradford City in an exchange deal involving reserve inside forward Ernie Tuckett.

1972   Two goals from Charlie George earned the Gunners maximum points in a 2–0 First Division win at home to title hopefuls Derby County.

13 February

1926   Arsenal secured a 3–0 First Division win over Newcastle United at Highbury with goals by Charlie Buchan, Billy Blyth and Dr James Paterson.

1956   Republic of Ireland international midfielder Liam Brady, capped 72 times, was born in Dublin. He netted 59 goals in 306 games for Arsenal.

1971   Ray Crawford scored twice as Colchester United gained a shock 3–2 FA Cup fifth-round victory at home to Leeds United.

1993   Ian Wright scored both goals as George Graham's side clinched a 2–0 FA Cup fifth-round win at home to Nottingham Forest.

1999   Holders Arsenal beat Sheffield United 2–1 in the FA Cup fifth round but in the interest of 'fair play' agreed to a historic rematch. Confused debutant Kanu had set up Marc Overmars' winner after United had kicked the ball into touch to allow an injured player to receive treatment.

14 February

1953 Sheffield Wednesday star Derek Dooley's career was ended by an injury against Preston North End, with his leg being subsequently amputated.

1973 Bobby Moore celebrated his 100th international appearance as he captained England's 5–0 win over Scotland at Hampden Park.

1985 Swiss international central defender Philippe Senderos was born in Geneva. He featured in Arsenal's 2005 FA Cup Final success.

1995 Dutch international striker Glenn Helder was signed from Vitesse Arnhem. He scored once in 39 Premiership games for Arsenal before being loaned to Benfica, then sold to NAC Breda.

1996 Former Liverpool manager Bob Paisley died aged 77. His glorious career at Anfield included three European Cup triumphs.

15 February

1934 England Under-23 forward Jimmy Bloomfield was born in Kensington, London. He scored 56 times in 227 appearances for the Gunners between 1954/55 and 1960/61 before moving to Birmingham City.

1936 Two goals by Ray Bowden plus another from Joe Hulme gave Arsenal a 3–3 FA Cup fifth-round draw at Newcastle United.

1992 Kevin Campbell and Anders Limpar netted two goals each in the Gunners' 7–1 First Division destruction of Sheffield Wednesday.

2003 Strikes by Edu and Sylvain Wiltord secured Arsenal a 2–0 FA Cup fifth-round victory over Manchester United at Old Trafford.

2004 Arsenal beat Chelsea for the fourth successive season in the FA Cup as Jose Antonio Reyes hit the target twice in a 2–1 fifth-round win.

16 February

1907 Arsenal inside forward Tim Coleman made his sole appearance for England in a 1–0 victory over Ireland at Goodison Park.

1952 Two goals by Reg Lewis plus another from Don Roper saw Arsenal to a nerve-tingling 3–3 First Division draw at home to Preston North End.

1955 England international winger Arthur Milton, capped only once, joined Bristol City. He netted 18 goals in 75 League games for Arsenal between 1950/51 and 1954/55.

1963 Johnny MacLeod, Laurie Brown and George Armstrong scored as Bolton Wanderers were put to the sword, 3–2 in a First Division encounter at Highbury.

2002 Sylvain Wiltord netted twice as the Gunners swept to an easy 5–2 FA Cup fifth-round victory at home to Gillingham.

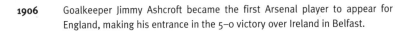

17 February

1906 Goalkeeper Jimmy Ashcroft became the first Arsenal player to appear for England, making his entrance in the 5–0 victory over Ireland in Belfast.

1932 Cliff Bastin, David Jack, Ray Parkin and Alex James registered in Arsenal's 4–0 First Division drubbing of Grimsby Town at Highbury.

1936 Republic of Ireland international winger Joe Haverty, who collected 32 caps, was born in Dublin. He scored 26 goals in 122 games for Arsenal.

1971 Charlie George netted twice to give Arsenal a 2–1 FA Cup fifth-round win over Manchester City at Maine Road on the Double trail.

1999 Nicolas Anelka's strike earned the Gunners a 1–1 Premiership draw against title rivals Manchester United at Old Trafford.

18 February

1928   Jimmy Brain scored twice as Herbert Chapman's side hit top gear in a 4–1 FA Cup fifth-round triumph at home to Aston Villa.

1953   Ray Daniel, Cliff Holton and Doug Lishman netted two goals each in Arsenal's 6–2 First Division home win over Derby County.

1965   Winger Terry Anderson was sold to Norwich City. He found the net six times in 25 First Division games for the Gunners.

1987   Arsenal central defender Tony Adams made his England international debut in the 4–2 victory over Spain in Madrid, and went on to score five times in 66 games.

2001   Substitute Sylvain Wiltord scored twice to secure the Gunners a 3–1 FA Cup fifth-round win over Chelsea at Highbury.

19 February

1905   Once-capped England centre half Herbie Roberts was born in Oswestry, Shropshire. He netted four goals in 297 League games for Arsenal between 1926/27 and 1937/38.

1916   Full back Bob Benson died in the dressing room after feeling unwell during Arsenal's 4–1 London Combination win over Reading. He had scored seven times in 52 League appearances for the Gunners.

1948   Scotland international wing-half Alex Forbes arrived at Highbury from Sheffield United. His illustrious Arsenal career was ended by a knee injury in 1955/56.

1980   Alan Sunderland registered twice as holders Arsenal gained a 3–0 FA Cup fifth-round replay win at home to Bolton Wanderers.

2005   Andy Gray's last-gasp penalty secured Sheffield United a 1–1 FA Cup fifth-round draw against Arsenal at Highbury.

20 February

1909   Albert Beney grabbed a hat-trick as George Morrell's side roared to a 5–0 First Division victory at home to Liverpool.

1937   Leading marksman Ted Drake netted four goals in Arsenal's 7–1 FA Cup fifth-round win over Burnley at Turf Moor.

1971   Charlie George, John Radford and Frank McLintock were on target in Arsenal's 3–2 First Division victory at home to Ipswich Town.

1988   Brian McClair missed a penalty as Mike Duxbury's own-goal gave Arsenal a 2–1 FA Cup fifth-round win over Manchester United.

1999   Nicolas Anelka scored his first hat-trick and Ray Parlour supplied two goals in Arsenal's 5–0 Premiership demolition of Leicester City at Highbury.

21 February

1931   Joe Hulme, David Jack, Jimmy Brain and Cliff Bastin scored in Arsenal's 4–1 First Division victory over Manchester United.

1964   Centre half Laurie Brown was sold to Tottenham Hotspur. He scored twice in 109 games during his Highbury career which began in 1961 after a transfer from Northampton Town.

1996   Arsenal lost on away goals after being held to a 0–0 draw at Aston Villa in the second leg of the Coca-Cola Cup semi-final.

2004   Arsène Wenger's side came from behind with goals by Patrick Vieira and Edu to clinch a 2–1 Premiership victory away to title rivals Chelsea.

2006   Cesc Fabregas shone as Thierry Henry's strike gave Arsenal a stunning 1–0 victory at Real Madrid in the UEFA Champions League.

22 February

1908   Inside forward Tim Coleman made his last Arsenal appearance as Charlie Lewis scored twice in a 4–1 First Division victory over Middlesbrough. Coleman had joined Arsenal in 1902 and scored 84 goals in 196 games.

1956   Newcastle United defeated Portsmouth 2–0 at Fratton Park in the first Football League match played under floodlights.

1975   Alan Ball and Bob McNab were sent off in Arsenal's 2–1 defeat at Derby County, the first double dismissal for the Club since December 1967.

1991   Kenny Dalglish resigned as Liverpool player-boss. He amassed a vast collection of honours as a player and manager while at Anfield.

2003   Dennis Bergkamp, Robert Pires, Thierry Henry, Sol Campbell and Patrick Vieira were all on target in the glittering 5–1 Premiership win at Manchester City.

23 February

1903   Northern Ireland international goalkeeper John Mackie was born in Monkstown. He made 108 League appearances for Arsenal, and collected three caps.

1929   Leading goalscorer David Jack netted as Herbert Chapman's team gained a 4–3 First Division win over West Ham United at Upton Park.

1965   Joe Baker scored Arsenal's one hundredth goal against Tottenham Hotspur in a 3–1 First Division victory over their local rivals at Highbury.

1991   David O'Leary, Paul Merson, Alan Smith and Kevin Campbell found the net in Arsenal's 4–0 First Division win at home to Crystal Palace.

1999   Eight Frenchmen took the field and Thierry Henry scored twice for leaders Arsenal in a 4–1 Premiership victory over Fulham.

24 February

1894   Walter Shaw contributed a hat-trick and Jim Henderson added two goals in the Gunners' 6–3 Second Division win at Middlesbrough Ironopolis, during the northern club's sole League campaign.

1906   Billy Garbutt netted twice as Phil Kelso's team cantered to a 5–0 FA Cup third-round victory at home to Sunderland.

1962   George Armstrong made his League debut as Geoff Strong's goal gave Arsenal a 1–0 First Division triumph at Blackpool.

1993   Former West Ham and England captain Bobby Moore died aged 51, just nine days after announcing he was suffering from cancer.

2004   Two goals by Edu plus another from Robert Pires lifted the Gunners to a 3–2 UEFA Champions League victory at Celta Vigo.

25 February

1933   Tim Coleman scored a hat-trick as championship-chasing Arsenal rampaged to an 8–0 First Division victory at home to Blackburn Rovers.

1950   Inside forward Noel Kelly made his League debut as Freddie Cox's goal clinched Arsenal's 1–0 First Division win at Everton.

1989   Goals from Perry Groves and Alan Smith secured leaders Arsenal a 2–0 First Division triumph over Luton Town at Kenilworth Road.

1995   Two goals by Chris Kiwomya plus another from Paul Merson saw the Gunners collect three points with a confident 3–0 Premiership win at Crystal Palace.

1998   First-half strikes by Nicolas Anelka and Dennis Bergkamp saw Arsenal to a 2–1 victory in a replayed FA Cup fifth-round encounter at Crystal Palace.

26 February

1927   Leading marksman Jimmy Brain scored four times in the Gunners' 6–2 First Division victory over Burnley at Highbury.

1966   England international centre forward Joe Baker, who won eight caps, joined Nottingham Forest. He rattled in 100 goals in 156 games for Arsenal between 1962/63 and 1965/66.

1979   Frank Stapleton's goal gave Arsenal a 1–0 FA Cup fifth-round win at Nottingham Forest, their first home defeat for 52 matches.

1983   Pat Jennings became the first player in England to appear in 1,000 senior matches, in Arsenal's 0–0 draw at West Bromwich Albion.

2000   Two goals by Freddie Ljungberg plus another from Dennis Bergkamp secured a 3–1 Premiership win at home to Southampton.

27 February

1904   Billy Gooing, Tommy Shanks and Tim Coleman were on the scoresheet in the Gunners' 3–0 Second Division victory at home to Barnsley.

1932   Herbie Roberts scored to give Arsenal a 1–0 FA Cup sixth-round win at Herbert Chapman's former club Huddersfield Town.

1937   Alf Kirchen netted his first hat-trick for Arsenal in the 3–1 First Division victory over Grimsby Town at Blundell Park.

1988   Two goals by Paul Merson plus others from Michael Thomas and Alan Smith gave Arsenal a 4–0 First Division win at home to Charlton Athletic.

2002   Robert Pires, Thierry Henry, Patrick Vieira and Dennis Bergkamp scored in Arsenal's 4–1 UEFA Champions League win over Bayer Leverkusen at Highbury.

28 February

1908   England international inside forward Tim Coleman, who earned one cap, moved to Everton. He netted 79 goals in 172 League games for Arsenal between 1902 and 1908.

1931   David Jack scored twice as title-chasing Arsenal completed a 4–2 First Division victory over West Ham United at Upton Park.

1953   Blackpool ended Arsenal's Double hopes as Ernie Taylor and Allan Brown scored in a 2–1 FA Cup sixth-round win at Highbury.

1983   Brian Talbot, Tony Woodcock and Paul Davis netted in the Gunners' 3–2 FA Cup fifth-round replay win at home to Middlesbrough.

2004   Early strikes by Robert Pires and Thierry Henry gave leaders Arsenal a 2–1 Premiership victory over Charlton Athletic at Highbury.

29 February

1904   Tommy Shanks grabbed a hat-trick as Harry Bradshaw's team surged to a 4–0 Second Division win at home to Burnley.

1908   Goals from Bert Freeman and Charlie Lewis gave the Gunners a 2–2 First Division draw against Sheffield United at Bramall Lane.

1924   Inside forward Jimmy Ramsay joined Arsenal from Kilmarnock. He netted 11 goals in 69 League games while at Highbury, then returned to Rugby Park.

1936   Pat Beasley scored twice as George Allison's side triumphed 4–1 at home to Barnsley in the FA Cup sixth round.

1972   Holders Arsenal drew 0–0 against League champions-elect Derby County in an FA Cup fifth-round replay at Highbury (see 13 March, page 44, for second replay).

1 March

1930   Two goals by Jack Lambert plus another from Alf Baker earned Arsenal a 3–0 FA Cup sixth-round win at West Ham United's Upton Park.

1935   Winger Alf Kirchen was signed from Norwich City. He netted 38 goals in 92 League outings while at Highbury, then retired due to injury.

1969   Leading marksman John Radford netted a hat-trick in Arsenal's 5–0 First Division demolition of Sheffield Wednesday at Hillsborough.

1987   Goals from Viv Anderson and Niall Quinn gave Arsenal a 2–1 Littlewoods Cup semi-final second-leg win at Tottenham Hotspur to level the tie at 2–2 (see 4 March, page 39, for replay).

2005   Arsenal defeated Sheffield United 4–2 on penalties after being held to a 0–0 FA Cup fifth-round replay draw at Bramall Lane.

2 March

1926   England right-back Tom Parker, who won his only cap against France in 1925, joined Arsenal from Southampton. He scored 17 times in 258 League games for the Club between 1925/26 and 1932/33.

1953   Cliff Holton scored four goals as Tom Whittaker's side gained a 4–1 First Division win over Sheffield Wednesday at Hillsborough.

1968   The Gunners made their first visit to Wembley for 16 years, but Terry Cooper's goal gave Leeds United a 1–1 win in the League Cup Final.

2000   Arsenal trounced Deportivo La Coruna 5–1 in the UEFA Cup fourth-round first leg, their first European success over a Spanish club.

2002   Arsenal, on the trail of the Double, gained a 2–0 Premiership victory at Newcastle United with highly-skilled goals from Dennis Bergkamp and Sol Campbell.

3 March

1906   Charlie Satterthwaite scored twice as Phil Kelso's team stormed to a 5–0 First Division victory at home to Birmingham City.

1928   Billy Blyth and Sid Hoar netted two goals apiece in Arsenal's 4–1 FA Cup sixth-round win over Stoke City at Highbury.

1939   England left half Wilf Copping, who collected 20 caps, rejoined Leeds United. He made 166 League appearances for Arsenal between 1934/35 and 1938/39.

1991   Arsenal completed the double over title rivals Liverpool, as Paul Merson's strike clinched a 1–0 First Division victory at Anfield.

2001   Sylvain Wiltord's first-half hat-trick secured Arsène Wenger's team a 3–0 Premiership victory at home to West Ham United.

4 March

1933   Arsenal wore their new strip, white sleeves on a red jersey, for the first time in a 1–0 First Division defeat at home to Liverpool after Herbert Chapman saw someone in the crowd wearing red and white.

1950   Tom Whittaker's team gained a 1–0 FA Cup sixth-round victory at home to Leeds United with a goal from Reg Lewis.

1967   Rodney Marsh inspired Third Division QPR to beat West Bromwich Albion 3–2 in the first League Cup Final staged at Wembley.

1987   Goals from Ian Allinson and David Rocastle gave the Gunners a 2–1 Littlewoods Cup semi-final replay win at Tottenham Hotspur, earning the right to face Liverpool at Wembley.

2006   Two goals by Thierry Henry plus others from Emmanuel Adebayor and Cesc Fabregas gave Arsenal a 4–0 Premiership win at Fulham.

5 March

1927   Arsenal triumphed 2–1 at home to Wolverhampton Wanderers in the FA Cup sixth round, thanks to goals by Billy Blyth and Jack Butler.

1938   Mal Griffiths scored twice as championship-chasing Arsenal swept to a 4–0 First Division victory over Stoke City at Highbury.

1980   Alan Sunderland netted a brace in Arsenal's 5–1 European Cup Winners' Cup third-round first-leg win at home to Gothenburg.

1994   Ian Wright grabbed a hat-trick as the Gunners romped to a 5–1 Premiership victory over Ipswich Town at Portman Road.

2005   Thierry Henry's first hat-trick of the season gave Arsène Wenger's team a 3–0 Premiership win at home to Portsmouth.

6 March

1935   Alf Kirchen scored twice on his debut as George Allison's side galloped to a 6–0 First Division victory at Tottenham Hotspur.

1962   Accrington Stanley admitted defeat in their fight for financial survival and resigned from the Football League. Results were expunged for season 1961/62 and they joined Lancashire Combination Division Two.

1993   Tony Adams netted his first goal of the campaign in Arsenal's 4–2 FA Cup sixth-round win over Ipswich Town at Portman Road.

1997   Arsenal signed 17-year-old striker Nicolas Anelka from Paris St Germain after a goodwill payment ended lengthy wrangling. Just over two years later he had gone to Real Madrid.

2004   Thierry Henry and Freddie Ljungberg netted two goals each in Arsenal's 5–1 FA Cup sixth-round victory at Portsmouth.

7 March

1891   The Gunners won their first trophy, defeating Medicos from St Bart's Hospital 6–0 in the London Senior Cup final at Kennington Oval.

1920   Inside forward Reg Lewis was born in Bilston, Staffordshire. He struck 103 goals in 154 First Division outings during his Highbury career, which began in 1936/37 and ended with retirement in 1953.

1928   Top scorer Jimmy Brain netted a hat-trick as Arsenal gained a 6–3 First Division victory over Liverpool at Highbury.

1990   Perry Groves, Tony Adams and Kevin Campbell scored in Arsenal's 3–0 First Division victory at home to Nottingham Forest.

2000   Tony Ford became the first English outfield player to reach 1,000 senior appearances in Rochdale's 1–0 win at Carlisle United.

8 March

1932   Wing-half Bill Seddon moved from Arsenal to Grimsby Town. He made 69 League appearances for the Gunners.

1958   David Herd netted a hat-trick as Jack Crayston's side squeezed out a dramatic 5–4 First Division victory over Chelsea at Highbury.

1980   Frank Stapleton scored twice as holders Arsenal secured a 2–1 FA Cup sixth-round win over Watford at Vicarage Road.

2003   First-half goals by Francis Jeffers and Thierry Henry earned the Gunners a 2–2 FA Cup sixth-round draw at home to Chelsea (see 25 March, page 50, for replay).

2006   Arsenal kept their sixth successive clean sheet in the UEFA Champions League as they drew 0–0 with Real Madrid, winning 1–0 on aggregate.

9 March

1929   Joe Hulme netted twice as Herbert Chapman's team powered to a 4–2 First Division victory over Liverpool at Anfield.

1935   Arsenal's 0–0 First Division draw with Sunderland was watched by 73,295, the record attendance for a match at Highbury.

1946   The Burnden Park disaster left 33 people dead as crush barriers collapsed during the FA Cup-tie between Bolton Wanderers and Stoke City.

1971   Goals from Frank McLintock and Peter Storey gave Arsenal, the holders, a 2–1 European Fairs Cup fourth-round first-leg win at home to Cologne (see 23 March, page 49, for second leg).

1991   Kevin Campbell and Tony Adams scored in the Gunners' 2–1 FA Cup sixth-round victory over Cambridge United at Highbury.

10 March

1906   A brace by Bert Freeman and a solo strike by Tim Coleman earned the Gunners a 3–2 FA Cup fourth-round win at Manchester United.

1964   England Under-23 wing-half cum inside forward John Barnwell joined Nottingham Forest. Later he played for Sheffield United before becoming a manager.

1993   Arsenal eased into the Coca-Cola Cup Final with two goals against Crystal Palace at Highbury for a 2–0 aggregate semi-final win (see 18 April, page 62, for final).

2000   England Under-21 midfielder Stephen Hughes was sold to Everton. He scored four times in 49 Premiership games for Arsenal.

2001   Sylvain Wiltord, Tony Adams and Robert Pires netted in the Gunners' 3–0 FA Cup sixth-round win at home to Blackburn Rovers.

11 March

1911   George Burdett and John Peart made their debuts as John Chalmers' goal clinched a 1–0 First Division win at home to Everton.

1970   Strikes by Jon Sammels and John Radford gave Arsenal a 2–0 Fairs Cup fourth-round first-leg win over Dinamo Bacau in Romania (see March 18, page 46, for second leg).

1978   Malcolm Macdonald, Alan Sunderland and Willie Young were on the mark in Arsenal's 3–2 FA Cup sixth-round victory at Wrexham.

1981   Midfielder Peter Nicholas, who accumulated a then-record 73 caps for Wales, joined the Club from Crystal Palace. He scored 3 goals in 80 games for Arsenal between 1980/81 and 1982/83.

1998   Chris Wreh scored his first goal in his first Premiership start as title-hunting Arsenal beat Wimbledon 1–0 at Selhurst Park.

12 March

1900   Ralph Gaudie grabbed a hat-trick as the Gunners stormed to a Club-record 12–0 victory over Loughborough Town at the Manor Ground.

1932   Arsenal made their sixth FA Cup semi-final appearance, with Cliff Bastin's goal clinching a 1–0 win over Manchester City.

1975   Alan Ball was captain as England celebrated their 100th international at Wembley by beating World champions West Germany 2–0.

1977   Arsenal lost their seventh successive League match, 2–1 to QPR at Loftus Road, the worst sequence in the Club's history.

2006   Thierry Henry scored twice in the Gunners' 2–1 Premiership victory over European Champions Liverpool at Highbury.

13 March

1926   Leading marksman Jimmy Brain grabbed a hat-trick as Arsenal carved out a fine 3–2 First Division win over Everton at Goodison Park.

1937   Two goals by Alf Kirchen plus others from Cliff Bastin and Ray Bowden earned Arsenal a tense 4–3 First Division win at Leeds United.

1970   Winger Jimmy Robertson was sold to Ipswich Town. He had kicked off his career with Cowdenbeath, developed at St Mirren and then thrived with Tottenham Hotspur before becoming a Gunner.

1972   Holders Arsenal gained a 1–0 FA Cup fifth-round second replay success over Derby County with a goal from Ray Kennedy.

2004   Second-half strikes by Thierry Henry and Robert Pires gave leaders Arsenal a 2–0 Premiership win at Blackburn Rovers.

14 March

1912   England international winger Cliff Bastin, who won 21 caps, was born in Exeter, Devon. He scored 150 times in 350 First Division games for the Gunners between 1929/30 and 1946/47 and remains the Club's 3rd highest goalscorer.

1934   The prolific Ted Drake joined Arsenal from Southampton. He netted 124 goals in 168 League outings during his Highbury stay.

1970   Strikes by Jon Sammels and John Radford gave Bertie Mee's side a 2–1 First Division victory at home to Liverpool.

1979   French international striker Nicolas Anelka was born in Versailles. He scored 23 times in 65 Premiership games for Arsenal between 1996/97 and 1998/99.

1998   Arsenal were back in the title race as Marc Overmars' goal clinched a vital 1–0 Premiership win at Manchester United.

15 March

1920   Billy Meredith became the oldest British international player in Wales' 2–1 win over England, in the first international match at Highbury.

1947   Reg Lewis' hat-trick plus a goal from Ronnie Rooke gave Arsenal a 4–1 First Division win at home to Preston North End.

1969   Don Rogers scored twice in extra time to earn Swindon Town a 3–1 triumph over Arsenal in the League Cup Final at Wembley.

1971   Arsenal reached their first FA Cup semi-final for 19 years after a 1–0 sixth-round replay win at home to Leicester City.

1990   Republic of Ireland international Niall Quinn, who accumulated 91 caps, joined Manchester City. He scored 20 goals in 93 games for Arsenal between 1985/86 and 1989/90.

16 March

1935   Goalkeeper Frank Moss scored, after being injured and returning on the wing, as title-chasing Arsenal triumphed 2–0 at Everton.

1956   England B international Doug Lishman joined Nottingham Forest. He scored 125 times in 226 League games for Arsenal between 1948/49 and 1955/56.

1957   Wycombe Wanderers reached Wembley for the first time with a 4–2 Amateur Cup semi-final win over Corinthian Casuals at Highbury.

1961   England Under-23 centre half Bill Dodgin was sold to Fulham. He made 191 First Division appearances during his time at Highbury.

1995   Arsenal reached the European Cup Winners' Cup semi-finals after Ian Wright's spectacular goal clinched a 1–0 win at Auxerre.

17 March

1923   Long-serving Arsenal left-half Bob John made his Welsh international debut in the 2–0 defeat by Scotland at Paisley. He went on to accumulate 15 caps.

1926   Jimmy Brain scored twice as Herbert Chapman's team surged to a 4–0 First Division victory at home to Sheffield United.

1949   Northern Ireland international right back Pat Rice was born in Belfast. He scored 13 times in 527 games for Arsenal between 1967/68 and 1980/81 and earned 49 caps before joning the Arsenal back-room staff in 1984.

1964   England international right back Lee Dixon was born in Manchester. He played for Burnley, Chester City, Bury and Stoke City before joining Arsenal in 1988.

1998   Dennis Bergkamp was sent-off but Arsenal defeated West Ham United 4–3 on penalties in the FA Cup sixth-round replay at Upton Park.

18 March

1899   Ernie Cottrell scored a hat-trick and Adam Haywood notched two goals in the Gunners' 6–0 Second Division crushing of Blackpool at Highbury.

1950   Arsenal came back with goals by Freddie Cox, direct from a corner, and Leslie Compton to clinch a 2–2 FA Cup semi-final draw with Chelsea.

1970   John Radford, Charlie George and Jon Sammels netted two goals each in a 7–1 European Fairs Cup fourth-round second-leg win over Dinamo Bacau at Highbury.

1972   Alan Ball scored to give holders Arsenal a 1–0 FA Cup sixth-round victory over giant-killers Orient at Brisbane Road. The Os had already knocked out Leicester City and Chelsea.

1979   Arsenal and Republic of Ireland midfielder Liam Brady was voted PFA Player of the Year, receiving the trophy at the London Hilton Hotel.

19 March

1923 Highbury became the first English ground to host a national team from an overseas country as England triumphed 6–1 in a friendly against Belgium.

1981 Ivory Coast international defender Kolo Touré was born in Mimosas. He featured in Arsenal's 2003/04 Premiership title triumph and their FA Cup glory in 2005.

1983 Top-scorer Tony Woodcock grabbed a hat-trick in Arsenal's 4–1 First Division victory over Luton Town at Highbury.

1994 Anders Limpar made his final appearance as Ian Wright netted a hat-trick in Arsenal's 4–0 Premiership win at Southampton.

2000 Gilles Grimandi was sent off but Thierry Henry's penalty clinched the Gunners' 2–1 Premiership win over Tottenham Hotspur at Highbury.

20 March

1926 Winger Jock Rutherford became the oldest player to appear for Arsenal at 41 years 159 days, in the 1–0 win at home to Manchester City.

1968 England international striker Paul Merson, who won 21 caps, was born in Harlesden, London. He netted 99 goals in 422 games for the Gunners between 1986/87 and 1996/97 before accepting a move to Middlesborough.

1976 Brian Kidd scored a hat-trick and Alan Ball added two goals in Arsenal's 6–1 First Division hammering of West Ham United at Highbury.

1993 Paul Dickov made his Premiership debut as Jimmy Carter netted twice in Arsenal's taut 4–3 victory at home to Southampton.

2004 First-half goals by Robert Pires and Dennis Bergkamp gave leaders Arsenal a 2–1 Premiership win at home to Bolton Wanderers.

21 March

1896   Centre half Caesar Jenkyns became the Gunners' first international when he featured in Wales' 4–0 defeat by Scotland at Dundee. His final cap tally was eight.

1903   Inside left Tommy Shanks became Arsenal's first Irish international when he played in the 2–0 win over Scotland in Glasgow. He went on to win two more caps.

1936   Cliff Bastin's strike gave George Allison's team a 1–0 FA Cup semi-final win over First Division rivals Grimsby Town.

1966   England Under-21 striker Martin Hayes was born in Walthamstow, London. He enjoyed his most successful campaign as a Gunner in 1986/87, when he scored 24 senior goals and helped to win the Littlewoods Cup.

1979   Charlie George made his debut for Southampton as Alan Sunderland scored twice in Arsenal's 2–0 FA Cup sixth-round replay win.

22 March

1930   Arsenal recovered with goals from David Jack and Cliff Bastin to secure a 2–2 FA Cup semi-final draw against Hull City.

1950   Arsenal booked a Wembley place to face Liverpool as Freddie Cox's extra-time strike clinched a 1–0 FA Cup semi-final replay victory over Chelsea.

1975   Two goals by Brian Hornsby plus another from Wilf Rostron gave Arsenal a 3–3 First Division draw at Burnley.

1986   Arsenal gained a 3–1 First Division win at home to Coventry City but the Gunners were rocked that day by the resignation of manager Don Howe.

1994   England Under-21 winger Neil Heaney was sold to Southampton. He had joined Arsenal in 1991 and made eight appearances for the Club.

23 March

1894 George Jacques and Jim Henderson scored two goals each in the Gunners' 6–0 Second Division home thrashing of Northwich Victoria.

1929 Jack Smith's goal gave Portsmouth a 1–0 victory over First Division rivals Aston Villa in the first FA Cup semi-final staged at Highbury.

1971 Arsenal lost their grip on the European Fairs Cup playing away to Cologne who won 0–1 with a late penalty in the fourth-round second leg.

2000 Ray Parlour grabbed a hat-trick as Arsenal triumphed 4–2 at Werder Bremen in the second leg of their UEFA Cup quarter-final (see 20 April, page 63, for semi-final).

2002 Robert Pires suffered a serious knee injury after scoring in Arsenal's 3–0 FA Cup sixth-round replay win over Newcastle United.

24 March

1934 Ted Drake scored on his debut as title-chasing Arsenal gained a 3–2 First Division win over Wolverhampton Wanderers at Highbury.

1962 Alan Skirton, John Barnwell and Johnny MacLeod netted in Arsenal's 3–2 First Division victory over Chelsea at Stamford Bridge.

1990 Kwame Ampadu made his League debut as Martin Hayes netted twice in the Gunners' 3–1 First Division victory at Derby County.

1994 Swedish international winger Anders Limpar was sold to Everton, with whom he would pocket an FA Cup winners' medal after shining in the 1995 final against Manchester United.

2004 Arsenal's 1–1 UEFA Champions League quarter-final first-leg draw at Chelsea, was their 17th consecutive match unbeaten against the Blues.

25 March

1939   Goals by Jock Anderson and Bert Barlow gave Portsmouth a 2–1 victory over Huddersfield Town in an FA Cup semi-final at Highbury.

1978   Malcolm Macdonald plundered his sole hat-trick of the season in Arsenal's 4–0 First Division win over West Bromwich Albion.

1988   Winger Brian Marwood was signed from Sheffield Wednesday. He played a key role in the Gunners' 1988/89 title triumph, creating countless chances for Alan Smith and company.

1989   Perry Groves, David Rocastle and Paul Merson hit the mark as championship-hunting Arsenal gained a 3–1 First Division victory at Southampton.

2003   Chelsea's John Terry scored for both sides as holders Arsenal triumphed 3–1 at Stamford Bridge in an FA Cup sixth-round replay.

26 March

1927   Arsenal reached their first Wembley final, where they would face Cardiff City, as Joe Hulme and Charlie Buchan netted in a 2–1 FA Cup semi-final win over Southampton.

1949   Portsmouth's Double hopes ended as Second Division strugglers Leicester City gained a shock 3–1 FA Cup semi-final win at Highbury.

1958   Alex Dawson netted a hat-trick as Manchester United defeated Fulham 5–3 in an FA Cup semi-final replay at Highbury.

1987   Striker Alan Smith was signed from Leicester City and was promptly loaned back to them for the remainder of the season.

2000   Goals from Thierry Henry, Gilles Grimandi and Kanu gave Arsenal a 3–0 Premiership victory at home to Coventry City.

27 March

1954   Two goals by Jimmy Logie plus another from Cliff Holton earned Arsenal a 3–1 First Division win at home to Manchester United.

1959   Centre half Jim Fotheringham was sold to Hearts. He made 72 First Division appearances during his Highbury tenure.

1971   Peter Storey scored twice, including a late penalty equaliser, as Arsenal came back to draw 2–2 with Stoke City in the FA Cup semi-final.

1982   Two goals by Graham Rix plus others from Alan Sunderland and Raphael Meade secured a 4–3 First Division win over Aston Villa at Highbury.

1997   Northern Ireland international Steve Morrow, who collected 39 caps, moved from Arsenal to QPR. He scored three times in 85 outings for the Gunners and also registered in a Wembley final (see 18 April, page 62).

28 March

1931   Jack Lambert scored a hat-trick and David Jack notched two goals as Arsenal gained a 5–2 First Division victory at Middlesbrough.

1970   George Graham netted twice to give Bertie Mee's side a 2–2 First Division draw at home to Wolverhampton Wanderers.

1992   Ray Parlour, Ian Wright and Kevin Campbell scored in the Gunners' 3–1 First Division victory over Wimbledon at Selhurst Park.

1998   Dennis Bergkamp's goal gave the Gunners, who were on the Double trail, a 1–0 Premiership win over Sheffield Wednesday at Highbury.

2006   Patrick Vieira returned with Juventus in the UEFA Champions' League quarter-final first leg as Arsenal triumphed 2–0 at Highbury.

29 March

1921   Joe North netted twice as Leslie Knighton's team gained a 4–3 First Division win over West Bromwich Albion at The Hawthorns.

1930   Two goals by Jack Lambert plus others from JJ Williams and Joe Hulme gave Arsenal a 4–0 First Division win over Blackburn Rovers at Highbury.

1958   Johnny Gordon scored twice as struggling Portsmouth scraped a 5–4 First Division victory over Arsenal at Highbury.

1973   Dutch international winger Marc Overmars was born in Ernst. He netted 40 goals in 141 outings for the Gunners between 1997/98 and 1999/2000 before leaving for Barcelona.

1994   Ian Wright's first-half strike gave Arsenal a 1–1 draw at Paris St Germain in the European Cup Winners' Cup semi-final first leg (see 12 April, page 59, for second leg).

30 March

1889   Preston North End became the first club to achieve the Double, with the Old Invincibles beating Wolves 3–0 in the FA Cup Final.

1929   Leading goalscorer David Jack netted four times as Herbert Chapman's team stormed to a 7–1 First Division win at home to Bury.

1935   Strikes by Pat Beasley, Ted Drake and Cliff Bastin gave title-chasing Arsenal a 3–1 First Division victory at Aston Villa.

1964   Alan Skirton grabbed a hat-trick as Billy Wright's side gained a 4–0 First Division win over Sheffield Wednesday at Hillsborough.

2002   Tony Adams made his 500th appearance as Patrick Vieira, Dennis Bergkamp and Sylvain Wiltord scored in a 3–0 Premiership win over Sunderland at Highbury.

31 March

1955   Arsenal goalkeeper Jack Kelsey made his Welsh international debut in a 0–0 draw against Ireland in a World Cup qualifier in Wrexham. He went on to win 41 caps.

1959   Welsh international centre forward Mel Charles joined Arsenal from Swansea Town along with Peter Davies and Dave Dodson.

1971   Double hopefuls Arsenal defeated Stoke City 2–0 in an FA Cup semi-final replay at Birmingham with goals from George Graham and Ray Kennedy.

1979   Goals by Frank Stapleton and Alan Sunderland gave Arsenal a 2–0 FA Cup semi-final victory over Wolverhampton Wanderers at Villa Park.

2001   In Arsène Wenger's 250th match in charge, which was dedicated to David Rocastle who died that day, Arsenal defeated Tottenham Hotspur 2–0.

1 April

1933   Jack Lambert scored twice as title-chasing Arsenal stormed to a 5–0 First Division victory over Aston Villa at Highbury.

1949   Northern Ireland left back Sammy Nelson, who collected 51 caps, was born in Belfast. He netted 12 goals in 338 outings for Arsenal between 1969/70 and 1980/81.

1978   Two goals by Malcolm Macdonald plus another from Liam Brady earned Arsenal a 3–1 First Division win at home to Manchester United.

1995   Welsh international John Hartson scored twice in the Gunners' comfortable 5–1 Premiership victory over Norwich City at Highbury.

2002   Arsenal returned to the top of the Premiership as Thierry Henry netted twice in a 3–0 win over Charlton Athletic at The Valley.

2 April

1906   Two goals by David Neave plus another from Bert Freeman gave the Gunners a 3–1 First Division win at home to Nottingham Forest.

1927   Arsenal winger Joe Hulme gained the first of his nine England caps in the 2–1 victory over Scotland in Glasgow.

1951   The first game played at Highbury under floodlights was the annual Boxers and Jockeys football match for the Sportsman's Aid Society.

1974   Goalkeeper Jimmy Rimmer was signed from Manchester United. Later in his career he helped Aston Villa to win the League title and European Cup.

2005   Thierry Henry's hat-trick plus a goal by Freddie Ljungberg gave Arsenal a 4–1 Premiership victory at home to Norwich City.

3 April

1899   England international inside forward David Jack, who won nine caps, was born in Bolton. He netted 113 goals in 181 League outings for the Gunners between 1928/29 and 1933/34.

1926   England international right back Tom Parker made his debut in Arsenal's 4–2 First Division win at home to Blackburn Rovers. He went on to captain the Gunners and lifted the FA Cup for them in 1932.

1979   Sammy Nelson scored, then dropped his shorts to celebrate, in Arsenal's 1–1 draw with Coventry City. He was banned for two matches.

1982   QPR reached their first FA Cup Final as Clive Allen's strike clinched a 1–0 semi-final win over West Bromwich Albion at Highbury.

1991   Kevin Campbell and Alan Smith netted two goals each as leaders Arsenal rampaged to a 5–0 First Division victory over Aston Villa at Highbury.

4 April

1903   Tim Coleman, Billy Linward and Billy Gooing each scored two goals in Arsenal's 6–1 Second Division win over Small Heath, who later became Birmingham City.

1929   Winger Mike Tiddy was born in Helston, Cornwall. He netted eight goals in 48 First Division outings while at Highbury.

1953   Don Roper scored twice as championship-chasing Arsenal gained a 5–3 First Division victory over Liverpool at Highbury.

1993   Arsenal reached their second final in a month, when Tony Adams' header clinched a 1–0 FA Cup semi-final win over Tottenham Hotspur (see 15 May, page 75).

2001   Strikes by Thierry Henry and Ray Parlour earned Arsenal a 2–1 victory at home to Valencia in the European Cup quarter-final first leg. The Gunners went out on the away-goals rule after losing 1–0 in Spain.

5 April

1902   A section of terracing collapsed during the match between Scotland and England at Ibrox Park, leaving 25 dead and over 500 injured.

1987   Arsenal recovered as two goals by Charlie Nicholas secured a 2–1 victory over Liverpool in the Littlewoods Cup Final at Wembley.

1992   Ten-man Liverpool snatched a last-gasp equalizer in extra time, to draw 1–1 against Portsmouth in the FA Cup semi-final at Highbury.

1998   Chris Wreh deputized for Dennis Bergkamp and scored in Arsenal's 1–0 FA Cup semi-final win over Wolverhampton Wanderers at Villa Park.

2006   Arsenal kept a record eighth successive clean sheet in Thierry Henry's 100th European game, as a 0–0 draw at Juventus eased them into the semi-finals of the UEFA Champions League.

6 April

1928   Joe Hulme, Charlie Buchan and Jimmy Brain registered in the Gunners' 3–0 First Division victory at home to Cardiff City.

1965   Tommy Baldwin made his League debut as Joe Baker, Alan Skirton and Frank McLintock scored in a 3–0 win over Birmingham City.

1991   Goals from Kevin Campbell and Alan Smith earned leaders Arsenal a 2–0 First Division victory over Sheffield United at Bramall Lane.

1995   Steve Bould scored twice in Arsenal's 3–2 European Cup Winners' Cup semi-final first-leg victory over Sampdoria at Highbury (see 20 April, page 63, for second leg).

2002   Lauren's late penalty gave leaders Arsenal a crucial 2–1 Premiership win at home to local rivals Tottenham Hotspur.

7 April

1900   Ralph Gaudie scored twice as Harry Bradshaw's team cruised to a 5–0 Second Division win at home to Merseyside club New Brighton Tower.

1952   Two goals by Freddie Cox plus another from Doug Lishman gave Arsenal a 3–0 FA Cup semi-final replay victory over Chelsea at Tottenham Hotspur.

1973   Arsenal failed to reach their third successive FA Cup Final as the Gunners lost 2–1 to Sunderland in the semi-final at Hillsborough.

1980   Paul Davis made his League debut as goals by Paul Vaessen and Alan Sunderland gave Arsenal a 2–1 win at Tottenham Hotspur. He went on to score 37 goals in 445 games for the Gunners between 1979/80 and 1994/95.

1984   Charlie Nicholas, Paul Mariner and Tony Woodcock scored in the Gunners' 3–1 First Division victory at home to Stoke City.

8 April

1933 Joe Hulme's hat-trick plus a goal from Cliff Bastin gave high-riding Arsenal a 4–3 First Division win at Middlesbrough.

1970 Two goals by Charlie George and a solo strike from Jon Sammels earned Arsenal a 3–0 win over Ajax in the first leg of the European Fairs Cup semi-final (see 15 April, page 60, for second leg).

1978 Ipswich Town reached their first FA Cup Final with a dramatic 3–1 semi-final victory over West Bromwich Albion at Highbury.

1990 In two thrilling FA Cup semi-finals, Crystal Palace beat Liverpool 4–3 and Oldham Athletic drew 3–3 with Manchester United.

2001 Strikes by Patrick Vieira and Robert Pires gave Arsène Wenger's side a 2–1 FA Cup semi-final victory over Tottenham Hotspur at Old Trafford.

9 April

1924 Wing-half Arthur Shaw was born in Limehouse, London. He made 57 First Division appearances during his tenure at Highbury, but scored no goals.

1955 Two goals by Don Roper plus another from Doug Lishman gave Arsenal a 3–0 First Division win at home to Blackpool.

1977 Arsenal gained a 2–0 First Division victory at West Bromwich Albion with goals by Malcolm Macdonald and Frank Stapleton.

1980 Roberto Bettega's own-goal enabled the Gunners to draw 1–1 against Juventus in the first leg of the European Cup Winners' Cup semi-final at Highbury (see 23 April, page 64, for second leg).

2004 Thierry Henry grabbed a stunning hat-trick as leaders Arsenal gained a 4–2 Premiership victory over Liverpool at Highbury.

10 April

1937 Preston North End reached their first FA Cup Final for 15 years with a 4–1 semi-final win over West Bromwich Albion at Highbury.

1948 Arsenal clinched their sixth League championship as Don Roper scored in a 1–1 First Division draw at Huddersfield Town.

1954 Derek Tapscott made his League debut and Joe Mercer his final appearance in Arsenal's 3–0 First Division win over Liverpool.

1970 Brian Kidd scored both goals as Manchester United beat Watford 2–0 in the first-ever FA Cup third-place play-off staged at Highbury.

1993 Arsenal gained a 2–1 Premier League win over Ipswich Town at Portman Road with goals from Alan Smith and Paul Merson.

11 April

1931 Wycombe Wanderers won the Amateur Cup for the first time as Alf Britnell's goal beat Hayes 1–0 in the final at Highbury.

1966 Tommy Baldwin netted twice in the Gunners' enthralling 4–4 First Division draw against West Bromwich Albion at The Hawthorns.

1992 Paul Merson's hat-trick plus a goal by Kevin Campbell gave Arsenal a 4–1 First Division victory at home to Crystal Palace.

1998 Arsenal brushed Newcastle United aside in a rehearsal for the FA Cup Final as Nicolas Anelka scored twice in a 3–1 Premiership win.

2001 Two goals by Freddie Ljungberg plus others from Sylvain Wiltord and Kanu furnished Arsenal with a crushing 4–0 Premiership win at Manchester City.

12 April

1895   Charlie Hare and Peter Mortimer netted two goals each in the Gunners' 6–1 Second Division win at home to Walsall Town Swifts, who were about to exit the League.

1930   Jack Lambert scored a hat-trick and Billy Johnstone grabbed a brace in Arsenal's crushing 8–1 First Division victory over Sheffield United at Highbury.

1964   Football was rocked when the *People* newspaper revealed three Sheffield Wednesday players had fixed a match to stage a betting coup.

1994   Arsenal reached the UEFA Cup Winners' Cup Final as Kevin Campbell's goal clinched a 1–0 win over Paris St Germain in the semi-final second-leg (see 4 May, page 70, for the final).

1997   Arsène Wenger's team gained a 2–0 Premiership victory at home to Leicester City with goals from Tony Adams and David Platt.

13 April

1936   Joe Payne scored a League record ten goals in Luton Town's 12–0 Third Division (South) victory at home to Bristol Rovers.

1971   Strikes by Frank McLintock, Ray Kennedy and Charlie George gave Arsenal a 3–0 First Division win at Nottingham Forest.

1974   Two goals by Ray Kennedy plus another from John Radford earned Bertie Mee's team a 3–1 First Division victory at Chelsea.

1997   Mark Hughes scored twice as eventual cup-winners Chelsea crushed Wimbledon 3–0 in the FA Cup semi-final at Highbury.

2003   David Seaman played his 1,000th senior match as Freddie Ljungberg supplied the winner in a 1–0 FA Cup semi-final win over Sheffield United.

14 April

1933 Joe Hulme netted twice as title-chasing Arsenal gained a crucial 4–2 First Division victory over Sheffield Wednesday at Highbury.

1934 Goalkeeper Frank Moss made his England international debut as Arsenal team-mate Cliff Bastin scored in a 3–0 win over Scotland. Moss went on to earn four caps, Bastin accumulated 21.

1936 Goalkeeper George Swindin was signed from Bradford City. He made 271 First Division appearances for the Gunners.

1984 Adrian Heath's extra-time winner gave Everton a 1–0 victory over Southampton in the FA Cup semi-final at Highbury.

2002 Gianluca Festa's own-goal gave Arsenal, who were chasing the Double, a 1–0 FA Cup semi-final win over Premiership rivals Middlesbrough at Old Trafford.

15 April

1961 Jimmy Greaves grabbed a hat-trick as England hammered Scotland 9–3 in the Home International at Wembley Stadium.

1970 Arsenal reached their first European final with a 3–1 aggregate win despite losing 1–0 at Ajax in the European Fairs Cup semi-final second leg.

1981 Eventual winners Tottenham Hotspur gained a 3–0 FA Cup semi-final replay victory over Wolverhampton Wanderers at Highbury.

1989 The Hillsborough disaster left 96 dead after a crowd surge at the FA Cup semi-final between Liverpool and Nottingham Forest.

1995 Ian Wright's hat-trick plus a goal by Paul Merson gave Arsenal a comfortable 4–1 Premiership victory at home to Ipswich Town.

16 April

1897 Hugh Cassidy made his sole League appearance as Paddy O'Brien scored twice in the Gunners' 5–1 Second Division win over Newcastle United.

1975 Malcolm Macdonald scored a record-equalling five goals as England beat Cyprus 5–0 in a European Championship qualifier.

1977 Swedish international midfielder Freddie Ljungberg was born in Vittsjo. He scored a terrific goal in the 2002 FA Cup Final victory over Chelsea, the first half of that season's Double (see 4 May, page 70).

1983 First Division strugglers Brighton and Hove Albion reached their first FA Cup Final with a 2–1 semi-final win over Sheffield Wednesday at Highbury.

2005 Robert Pires' goal and two late strikes by Robin van Persie secured the Gunners' 3–0 FA Cup semi-final win over Blackburn Rovers at the Millennium Stadium.

17 April

1892 Centre forward Bert White was born in Watford. He netted 40 goals in 101 First Division games for the Gunners between 1919 and 1922, then went on to join Blackpool.

1926 Bert Lawson, Joe Hulme and Tom Parker scored in Arsenal's 3–1 First Division win at home to title rivals Huddersfield Town.

1937 Denis Compton scored twice as George Allison's side racked up a 4–0 First Division victory over Portsmouth at Highbury.

1985 Goals from Charlie Nicholas and Brian Talbot saw the Gunners through to a 2–0 First Division win at Tottenham Hotspur.

1995 John Hartson and Ian Wright netted two goals apiece in Arsenal's easy 4–0 Premiership win at struggling Aston Villa.

18 April

1903   Bury gained a record 6–0 FA Cup Final win over Derby County. The Shakers did not concede a goal in the competition that season.

1927   Herbie Roberts made his League debut as Bob John scored twice in Arsenal's 3–2 First Division victory at Aston Villa.

1931   Arsenal won the First Division League Championship for the first time as goals by Jack Lambert, Cliff Bastin and David Jack beat Liverpool 3–1.

1993   Goals by Paul Merson and Steve Morrow, who was injured during the final whistle celebration, secured a 2–1 win over Sheffield Wednesday in the Coca-Cola Cup Final.

1998   Nigel Winterburn played his 500th game for Arsenal as the Gunners went top of the Premiership with a 5–0 win over Wimbledon. He went on to play 583 games for Arsenal between 1987/88 and 1999/2000.

19 April

1935   Ted Drake scored his seventh hat-trick of the campaign as Arsenal swept to an 8–0 First Division victory at home to Middlesbrough.

1947   Leytonstone won the Amateur Cup for the first time, beating Isthmian League rivals Wimbledon 2–1 in the final at Highbury.

1974   Arsenal goalkeeper Bob Wilson announced his retirement. He would finish playing at the end of the season and go on to work for the BBC.

1994   Arsenal were held to a 1–1 draw by Wimbledon at Highbury, the last time the Gunners started with an all-English team in the League.

2006   Kolo Touré's goal shortly before half time gave Arsenal a 1–0 win at home to Villarreal in the UEFA Champions League semi-final first-leg.

20 April

1929   Ilford won the Amateur Cup for the first time, beating holders Leyton 3–1 in the first Amateur Cup Final staged at Highbury.

1964   Ex-England Youth right back Dave Bacuzzi joined Manchester City. He made 48 appearances for Arsenal after joining the Club in 1961.

1995   Holders Arsenal defeated Sampdoria 3–2 on penalties after a thrilling 5–5 draw on aggregate in the UEFA Cup Winners' Cup semi-final played at Sampdoria.

2000   Arsenal reached their first European final for five years as Kanu's late winner clinched a 2–1 UEFA Cup semi-final second-leg win at Lens.

2002   Arsenal's sidelined French international winger Robert Pires was voted Footballer of the Year, pipping Ruud van Nistelrooy.

21 April

1930   David Halliday scored four goals and Cliff Bastin added two in Arsenal's stunning 6–6 First Division draw against Leicester City at Filbert Street – the Club's highest scoring away draw.

1964   England international right back Don Howe arrived at Highbury from West Bromwich Albion. He scored once in 74 games for Arsenal and went on to manage the Gunners from 1983 to 1986.

1971   Arsenal midfielder Peter Storey gained the first of his 19 England caps in the 3–0 victory over Greece at Wembley.

1984   Charlie Nicholas netted a brilliant solo goal in Arsenal's 3–2 First Division victory over Tottenham Hotspur at Highbury.

2001   Freddie Ljungberg, Gilles Grimandi, Sylvain Wiltord and Thierry Henry all registered in Arsenal's 4–1 Premiership win over Everton.

22 April

1908   Scotland international full-back Jimmy Sharp, who won five caps, joined Glasgow Rangers. He scored four times in 103 League games for Arsenal between 1905 and 1908.

1912   John Grant scored a hat-trick and John Flanagan netted twice in Arsenal's 5–1 First Division win at home to Blackburn Rovers.

1933   Arsenal clinched the League title for the second time in three years with a 3–1 victory at Chelsea.

1978   John Devine made his League debut as Paul Hart netted an own-goal in Arsenal's 3–1 First Division win at Leeds United.

1998   Arsenal central defender Tony Adams gained his 50th England cap in the 3–0 victory over Portugal at Wembley.

23 April

1913   Inside forward Bobby Davidson was born in Lochgelly, Fifeshire. He netted 13 goals in 57 First Division games while at Highbury.

1927   First Division rivals Cardiff City defeated Arsenal 1–0 in the FA Cup Final after an error by goalkeeper Dan Lewis.

1980   Paul Vaessen's late strike clinched Arsenal's 1–0 win (2–1 on aggregate) at Juventus in the European Cup Winners' Cup semi-final second leg.

1995   In the first Wembley final to be decided by a golden goal, Paul Tait gave Birmingham City a 1–0 extra-time victory over Carlisle United.

2000   Two goals by Thierry Henry plus another from Ray Parlour gave the Gunners a 3–2 Premiership victory at Watford.

24 April

1915   Havry King scored four goals as Arsenal charged to a 7–0 home mauling of Nottingham Forest in the Gunners' last game played outside the top flight.

1974   Jimmy Rimmer made his debut as Ray Kennedy's goal gave Bertie Mee's side a 1–0 First Division victory at Liverpool.

1988   Andy Dibble saved Nigel Winterburn's penalty at a crucial stage as Luton Town defeated Arsenal 3–2 in the Littlewoods Cup Final.

1999   Nicolas Anelka and Kanu netted two goals apiece as Arsenal triumphed 6–0 at Middlesbrough, their best away win for 40 years.

2002   Late strikes by Freddie Ljungberg and Kanu gave Arsenal, who were hunting the Double, a 2–0 Premiership win over West Ham United at Highbury.

25 April

1914   Burnley beat Liverpool 1–0 in the First FA Cup final to be attended by the sovereign, King George V, and the last held at Crystal Palace.

1936   Arsenal won the FA Cup for the second time as Ted Drake's goal clinched a 1–0 win over Sheffield United in the Wembley final.

1964   Jim Fryatt scored the fastest goal in first-class football, netting for Bradford PA against Tranmere Rovers after just four seconds.

2004   Arsenal clinched the Premiership title as Patrick Vieira and Robert Pires scored in a 2–2 draw at Tottenham Hotspur.

2006   Arsenal reached their first UEFA Champions League Final after Jens Lehmann saved Juan Riquelme's late penalty in a 0–0 draw at Villarreal.

26 April

1930   Arsenal won the FA Cup for the first time as Jack Lambert and Alex James netted in a 2–0 win over Huddersfield Town at Wembley.

1947   Leading marksman Reg Lewis scored four times in Arsenal's 5–3 First Division victory over Grimsby Town at Highbury.

1971   Jack Charlton's injury-time goal gave title rivals Leeds United a 1–0 First Division win at home to Arsenal, who were still chasing the Double.

1975   Brian Kidd's first-half strike clinched the Gunners' 1–0 First Division victory at home to relegation-threatened Tottenham Hotspur.

1993   Legendary manager Brian Clough announced his retirement, with Nottingham Forest facing relegation from the top-flight.

27 April

1898   England international wing-half Alf Baker was born in Ilkeston, Derbyshire. He netted 23 goals in 310 League outings for the Gunners between 1919/20 and 1930/31, then retired.

1904   Forward Charlie Satterthwaite was signed from West Ham United. He scored 45 times in 129 League games for the Gunners, starting in 1904/05 and finishing in 1909/10.

1909   Two goals by Harry Lee plus others from Tom Fitchie and Charlie Lewis secured a 4–1 First Division win at Manchester United.

1974   Manchester United were relegated after Denis Law's late winner against his former club gave Manchester City a 1–0 victory at Old Trafford.

2003   Ace marksman Thierry Henry was voted PFA Player of the Year. The PFA's Premiership team contained five Arsenal players.

28 April

1923   Bolton Wanderers beat West Ham United 2–0 in the first FA Cup Final at Wembley when a policeman on a white horse famously restored crowd order.

1965   Special benefit match for Sir Stanley Matthews between Stoke City and an International XI. He was the first footballer to be knighted.

1970   Bertie Mee's side lifted the European Fairs Cup as a 3–0 second-leg win at home to Anderlecht in the final clinched a rousing 4–3 aggregate victory.

1980   Alan Sunderland scored Arsenal's fastest FA Cup goal, after just 13 seconds, in the 1–1 semi-final second-replay draw against Liverpool (see 1 May, page 68, for third replay).

1984   Former Arsenal player and coach Don Howe, who had been caretaker-boss after Terry Neill's sacking, was appointed manager.

29 April

1912   George Morrell's side gained a 3–0 victory over Tottenham Hotspur in the Titanic Disaster Fund match staged at White City.

1939   Portsmouth gained a shock 4–1 victory over Wolverhampton Wanderers in the last FA Cup Final before the Second World War.

1950   Arsenal won the FA Cup for the third time as Reg Lewis scored both goals in a 2–0 win over Liverpool in the Wembley final.

1967   Colin Addison, George Graham, George Armstrong and Peter Simpson all netted in Arsenal's 4–1 First Division win at Burnley.

2002   First-half goals from Freddie Ljungberg and Sylvain Wiltord earned leaders Arsenal a 2–0 Premiership win at Bolton Wanderers.

30 April

1932 Cliff Bastin and Jack Lambert scored two goals each as Herbert Chapman's side eased to a 5–0 First Division win over Middlesbrough.

1952 British Olympic XI played an England B Trial XI at Highbury.

1969 Central defender John Roberts joined Arsenal from Northampton Town. He scored five times in 81 outings while at Highbury from 1969/70 to 1972/73 before transferring to Birmingham City.

1984 Scotland inside-forward Jimmy Logie, 64, died in London. He netted 68 goals in 296 League games for the Gunners between 1946/47 and 1954/55, and made one appearance for Scotland.

2005 Chelsea clinched the Premiership title, their first Championship success for 50 years, with a 2–0 victory at Bolton Wanderers.

1 May

1943 Reg Lewis netted four goals as Arsenal trounced Charlton Athletic 7–1 in the wartime Football League Cup South Final at Wembley.

1953 Arsenal defeated Burnley 3–2 to pip Preston North End on goal average to win the League title for the seventh time.

1974 Sir Alf Ramsey was sacked as England manager. He had engineered the 1966 World Cup victory during an 11-year reign.

1980 Arsenal reached their third successive FA Cup Final as Brian Talbot's goal clinched a 1–0 semi-final third-replay win over Liverpool.

1976 Southampton won the FA Cup for the first time as Bobby Stokes' late goal clinched a 1–0 victory over Manchester United.

2 May

1931 Second Division high-fliers West Bromwich Albion became the only club ever to achieve a promotion and FA Cup Double.

1953 Stan Mortensen netted an FA Cup hat-trick as Blackpool beat Bolton Wanderers 4–3 in the 'Matthews final' at Wembley.

1958 Republic of Ireland international David O'Leary, capped 68 times, was born in Stoke Newington, London. Between 1975/76 and 1992/93 he netted 14 goals in 722 games, which remains the Arsenal appearance record.

1967 England international midfielder David Rocastle was born in Lewisham, London. He scored 34 times in 275 games for the Gunners between 1985/86 and 1991/92, and won 14 caps.

1992 Top scorer Ian Wright grabbed a hat-trick as fourth-placed Arsenal ended the First Division campaign with a 5–1 win at home to Southampton.

3 May

1950 Footballing cricketer Denis Compton, aged 31, made his final appearance for the Gunners in a 2–0 First Division victory at home to champions Portsmouth.

1951 The Meteropolitan Police played the Paris Police in a match at Highbury.

1965 Danish international midfielder John Jensen was born in Copenhagen. He scored once in 98 Premiership games for Arsenal between 1992/93 and 1995/96.

1971 Arsenal won their eighth League crown as Ray Kennedy's late header clinched a 1–0 victory at Tottenham Hotspur.

1998 Arsenal sealed the Premiership title as Marc Overmars scored twice and Tony Adams' volley completed a 4–0 win at home to Everton.

4 May

1962   Goalkeeper Ian McKechnie moved to Southend United. He made 25 appearances while at Highbury after joining the Gunners in 1961.

1987   Spanish Under-21 international midfielder Cesc Fabregas was born in Barcelona. He featured in Arsenal's 2005 FA Cup Final triumph (see 21 May, page 78).

1994   Without the suspended Ian Wright, a determined Arsenal beat Parma 1–0 in the European Cup Winners' Cup Final with a great volleyed goal by Alan Smith.

2002   Ray Parlour and Freddie Ljungberg scored two stunning individual goals to give Arsenal a 2–0 victory over Chelsea in the FA Cup Final.

2004   Jose Antonio Reyes netted a second-half equalizer as Premiership champions Arsenal gained a 1–1 draw at Portsmouth.

5 May

1951   Father Alec (39) and son David Herd (17) played in the same Stockport County team that won 2–0 at Hartlepools United.

1956   Goalkeeper Bert Trautmann played on with a broken neck as Manchester City defeated Birmingham City 3–1 in the FA Cup Final.

1966   Arsenal's 3–0 First Division defeat by Leeds United was watched by a crowd of 4,554, the lowest attendance for a League match at Highbury.

1990   David O'Leary passed George Armstrong's record of 500 League appearances in Arsenal's 2–2 First Division draw at Norwich City.

1996   Arsenal qualified for the UEFA Cup as late goals by David Platt and Dennis Bergkamp defeated Bolton Wanderers 2–1 at Highbury.

6 May

1914   Inside forward Billy Blyth was signed from Manchester City. He netted 45 goals in 314 League outings for the Gunners between 1914/15 and 1928/29.

1939   Footage from Arsenal's 2–0 First Division victory at home to Brentford was used in the film *The Arsenal Stadium Mystery*.

1961   Tottenham Hotspur clinched the first Double of the 20th century, beating Leicester City 2–0 in the FA Cup final.

1991   Alan Smith grabbed a hat-trick as newly crowned champions Arsenal gained a 3–1 First Division win over Manchester United.

2000   Thierry Henry scored twice as Arsène Wenger's side secured a 2–1 Premiership victory over Chelsea at Highbury.

7 May

1883   Right back Joe Shaw was born in Bury, Lancashire. He made 309 League appearances for the Gunners and later went on to become reserve-team manager and caretaker manager of the first team following Herbert Chapman's death in 1934.

1931   Winger Pat Beasley was signed from non-League Stourbridge. He scored 19 times in 79 First Division outings while at Highbury.

1938   Arsenal clinched the League crown for the fifth time in eight years with an emphatic 5–0 victory at home to Bolton Wanderers.

2003   In an FA Cup Final rehearsal, Jermaine Pennant and Robert Pires scored Premiership hat-tricks as Arsenal beat Southampton 6–0; the first time two players from the same side had scored a hat-trick in a Premiership match.

2006   Thierry Henry scored a hat-trick in the 4–2 win over Wigan in the last ever game at Highbury, securing Arsenal the fourth and final UEFA Champions League place.

8 May

1910　England international right back George Male, who was capped 19 times, was born in West Ham. He made 285 First Division appearances for Arsenal.

1942　Northern Ireland international Terry Neill was born in Belfast. He netted ten goals in 275 games for the Gunners, making his debut in 1960 and bowing out in 1970, and won 59 caps.

1971　Arsenal completed the Double, making a sensational comeback through goals by Eddie Kelly and Charlie George to stun Liverpool, beating the Reds 2–1 in the FA Cup Final.

2002　Arsenal again clinched the Double, remaining unbeaten away from home in the League, as Sylvain Wiltord's strike secured a 1–0 win at Manchester United.

2006　Arsenal's 17-year-old striker Theo Walcott was a shock call-up for England's World Cup squad, along with Ashley Cole and Sol Campbell.

9 May

1931　Welsh international goalkeeper Dan Lewis moved to Gillingham. He made 142 First Division appearances for Arsenal.

1936　Arsenal centre half Bernard Joy was the last amateur player to appear in a full England international in the 3–2 defeat in Belgium.

1954　Arsenal inside forward Derek Tapscott made his Welsh international debut in the 2–0 defeat by Austria in Vienna.

2000　Goals from Lee Dixon, Silvinho and Thierry Henry gave the Gunners a 3–3 Premiership draw at home to Sheffield Wednesday.

2004　Arsenal's 1–0 victory at Fulham was their 29th successive unbeaten match in domestic competition against London opposition.

10 May

1899   Scottish left back Jimmy Jackson was signed from Newcastle United. He made 183 League appearances for the Gunners.

1941   Denis Compton's goal gave Arsenal a 1–1 draw against Preston North End in the Football League War Cup Final at Wembley.

1980   Trevor Brooking's first-half header earned West Ham United a 1–0 victory over holders Arsenal in the FA Cup Final.

1995   Nayim's goal in the last minute of extra time gave Real Zaragoza a 2–1 triumph over Arsenal in the European Cup Winners' Cup Final.

2004   Arsenal striker Thierry Henry was voted Footballer of the Year for the second consecutive season. He also won the Professional Footballers Association award.

11 May

1968   Manchester City pipped rivals Manchester United to the League Championship after winning 4–3 at Newcastle United.

1985   Bradford City's Third Division title celebrations ended in disaster as a fire in the main stand at Valley Parade killed 56 people.

1991   Anders Limpar netted his first hat-trick for Arsenal as the League champions trounced Coventry City 6–1 at Highbury.

1998   After leading Arsenal to the Double, Arsène Wenger was named Carling Manager of the Year, the first Arsenal boss to receive the honour.

2002   In a carnival atmosphere, Arsenal wrapped up their Double campaign with an entertaining 4–3 Premiership win at home to Everton.

12 May

1908   Winger Jackie Mordue joined Sunderland. He scored once in 26 League games for Arsenal and later won two England caps.

1922   Centre half George Pattison moved from Arsenal to West Ham United. He played nine First Division games for the Gunners.

1945   England World Cup-winning midfielder Alan Ball, who was capped 72 times, was born in Farnworth, Lancashire. He netted 52 goals in 217 outings for Arsenal between 1971/72 and 1976/77.

1979   Alan Sunderland's dramatic last-gasp strike gave Arsenal an unforgettable 3–2 victory over Manchester United in the FA Cup Final.

2001   Two stunning late goals from Michael Owen earned Liverpool a 2–1 win over Arsène Wenger's side in the first FA Cup Final at the Millennium Stadium.

13 May

1904   Scotland international right back 'Baldie' Gray was signed from Hibernian. He made 184 League appearances for the Gunners.

1908   Centre forward Sam Raybould was recruited from Sunderland. He netted six goals in 25 League outings for the Gunners, all during the 1908/09 campaign.

1933   Arsenal left back Eddie Hapgood made his England international debut as Cliff Bastin's goal clinched a 1–1 draw against Italy in Rome.

1967   Arsenal finished seventh in the First Division after George Graham scored in a 1–1 draw against Sheffield Wednesday at Hillsborough.

2002   Tony Adams, 19 years a Gunner and fresh from captaining Arsène Wenger's side to the Double, enjoyed a second testimonial, against Scottish champions Celtic at Highbury.

14 May

1935 Welsh international Mel Charles, who accumulated 31 caps, was born in Swansea. He netted 28 goals in 64 games for the Gunners between 1959/60 and 1961/62.

1980 Terry Neill's side lost 5–4 on penalties after a 0–0 draw against Valencia in the European Cup Winners' Cup Final played in Brussels.

1986 Ex-Arsenal player George Graham, a Double winner in 1970/71, returned to Highbury as manager in succession to Don Howe.

1988 Skipper Dave Beasant saved a penalty and Lawrie Sanchez's goal gave Wimbledon a 1–0 win over Liverpool in the FA Cup Final.

1995 Kenny Dalglish's Blackburn Rovers won the Premiership title, their first Championship for 81 years, despite losing 2–1 at Liverpool.

15 May

1949 Doug Lishman scored four goals as Arsenal started their Brazilian tour with a 5–1 win over Fluminense in Rio de Janeiro.

1982 Two goals by Paul Davis plus others from Stewart Robson and John Hawley gave Arsenal a 4–1 First Division win over Southampton at Highbury.

1990 England goalkeeper David Seaman, who turned out in 75 internationals, joined Arsenal from QPR. He made 560 appearances during his glorious Highbury sojourn stretching from 1990/91 to 2002/03.

1993 Ian Wright's first-half strike gave George Graham's side a 1–1 draw against Sheffield Wednesday in the FA Cup Final (see 20 May, page 78, for replay).

2004 Arsenal the Invincibles! The champions completed an unbeaten Premiership campaign as they came from behind to defeat Leicester City 2–1 at Highbury.

16 May

1934   England right half Jack Crayston, who was awarded eight caps, was signed from Bradford Park Avenue. He netted 16 goals in 168 League outings for the Gunners between 1934/35 and 1939/40.

1980   Strikes by Steve Walford and Frank Stapleton gave Arsenal a 2–1 First Division victory over Wolverhampton Wanderers at Molineux.

1987   Coventry City won the FA Cup for the first time as they came from behind to defeat Tottenham Hotspur 3–2 at Wembley.

1998   Arsenal clinched their second Double as Marc Overmars and Nicolas Anelka netted in a 2–0 FA Cup Final win over Newcastle United at Wembley.

1999   Arsène Wenger's team finished as Premiership runners-up after Kanu's strike clinched a 1–0 victory over Aston Villa at Highbury.

17 May

1929   Teenage winger Cliff 'Boy' Bastin arrived from Exeter City. He played a leading role as the Gunners lifted five League crowns and won the FA Cup twice.

1993   Record appearance holder David O'Leary, 20 years at Arsenal, scored in his testimonial against Manchester United at Highbury.

2000   Arsenal lost 4–1 on penalties in the UEFA Cup Final as Galatasaray became the first Turkish side to win a European trophy.

2003   In the first FA Cup Final to be played beneath a closed roof, Robert Pires scored as Arsenal retained the trophy with a 1–0 victory over Southampton at the Millennium Stadium.

2006   Jens Lehmann was sent off for a professional foul as Arsenal lost 2–1 to Barcelona in the UEFA Champions League Final in Paris.

18 May

1899   Diminutive winger Jim Tennant was signed from non-League St Bernards. He netted eight goals in 51 League games for the Gunners.

1928   Welsh international winger Charlie Jones, who won eight caps, joined from Nottingham Forest. He scored eight times in 176 League games for Arsenal.

1930   Left back Dennis Evans was born in Ellesmere Port, Cheshire. He was both versatile and athletic, once deputizing between the posts for injured goalkeeper Jack Kelsey during an FA Cup tie.

1969   Dutch international striker Dennis Bergkamp was born in Amsterdam. He starred for Arsenal in three Premiership title triumphs.

2005   Arsenal won the FA Cup for the tenth time, beating holders Manchester United 5–4 on penalties after a 0–0 draw in the final.

19 May

1910   Woolwich Arsenal narrowly avoided being taken over by Fulham after Sir Henry Norris bought a controlling interest in the Club, but the League committee vetoed Norris' plan to join the two clubs.

1932   Scotland international wing-half Frank Hill, who earned three caps, arrived from Aberdeen. He netted four goals in 76 League games for Arsenal.

1976   Ex-England Youth midfielder Brian Hornsby left Highbury to join Shrewsbury Town. He scored six times in 26 outings for Arsenal.

1977   Goalkeeper Manuel Almunia was born in Pamplona, Spain. He was a member of Arsenal's 2005 FA Cup-winning squad.

2001   Southampton said a nostalgic farewell to The Dell as Matt Le Tissier's late goal clinched a 3–2 Premiership victory over Arsenal.

20 May

1963   Alan Skirton scored twice as Arsenal drew 2–2 against Glasgow Rangers in Jack Kelsey's testimonial match at Highbury.

1964   Joe Baker and George Armstrong each grabbed a brace in the Gunners' 5–1 friendly win over Western Province in Cape Town.

1977   Malcolm Macdonald plundered a hat-trick as Arsenal ended their three-match Norwegian tour with a 6–0 friendly victory over Roros.

1993   Andy Linighan's thunderous header in extra time clinched Arsenal's 2–1 victory over Sheffield Wednesday in the FA Cup Final replay at Wembley.

1997   England Under-21 defender Matthew Rose was sold to QPR. He made five Premiership appearances while at Highbury from 1995 to 1997.

21 May

1897   Centre forward Fergus Hunt was signed from Lancashire club Darwen, a fellow Second Division outfit. He netted 30 goals in 72 League games during two spells with the Gunners.

1923   Arsenal goalkeeper Ernie Williamson gained the first of his two England caps in the 4–2 victory over Sweden in Stockholm.

1956   England Youth defender Richie Powling was born in Barking, London. He netted three goals in 55 First Division games for Arsenal between 1973 and 1978.

1966   Cassius Clay (later Muhammad Ali) defeated Henry Cooper in the sixth-round of a World heavyweight boxing match staged at Highbury.

2005   The Gunners lifted the FA Cup for the tenth time, beating Manchester United 5–4 on penalties after a 0–0 draw. The winning kick was Patrick Vieira's last in an Arsenal shirt.

22 May

1902   Centre forward Jack Lambert was born in Greasbrough, Yorkshire. He netted 98 goals in 143 First Division games for the Gunners between 1926 and 1933 .

1914   Centre half Chris Buckley was signed from Aston Villa. He scored three times in 56 League outings for Arsenal between 1914 and 1920.

1946   Welsh international winger Les Jones joined Swansea Town as player-coach. He netted three goals in 46 League outings for Arsenal.

1953   England striker Paul Mariner, capped 35 times, was born in Bolton. He started his career with Plymouth Argyle, rose to prominence with Ipswich Town, then served Portsmouth after leaving Highbury in 1986.

1971   Arsenal skipper Frank McLintock won his ninth and last cap for Scotland in the 3–1 defeat by England at Wembley.

23 May

1918   Footballing cricketer Denis Compton was born in Hendon, London. He netted five goals in 253 First Division games for Arsenal and played in 78 Test matches for England.

1942   Winger Alf Kirchen's strike gave Arsenal a 1–1 draw in a wartime friendly against the RAF XI at Highbury.

1948   Arsenal wing-half Archie Macaulay won his seventh and last cap for Scotland in the 3–0 defeat by France in Paris.

1968   Goals from Bobby Gould, John Radford and Terry Neill earned Arsenal a 3–1 friendly win over a Japan XI in Tokyo.

1993   Port Vale made the first of two visits to Wembley in a week, beating Stockport County 2–1 in the Autoglass Trophy final.

24 May

1899   Left back Horace Cope was born in Treeton, near Sheffield. He made 65 First Division appearances while at Highbury between 1926 and 1933.

1939   Reg Lewis' hat-trick plus a goal by Gordon Bremner gave the Gunners a 4–1 friendly win over a Danish XI in Copenhagen.

1947   Goals from Jack Balmer and Bob Priday earned title-chasing Liverpool a 1–2 First Division victory over Arsenal at Highbury.

1967   Colin Addison scored twice as Bertie Mee's team swept to a 7–0 friendly win over Apollon/AEL Select in Limassol, Cyprus.

1975   Arsenal midfielder Alan Ball played his 72nd and last game for England in the 5–1 victory over Scotland at Wembley.

25 May

1928   Two goals by Joe Hulme plus another from Archie Clark gave Arsenal a 3–2 friendly victory over Helsingborg in Sweden.

1952   Nat Lofthouse was dubbed 'Lion of Vienna' after scoring twice in England's 3–2 win against Austria who, at the time, were rated the best team in Europe.

1967   Jock Stein's Celtic became the first British team to win the European Cup, beating Inter Milan 2–1 in the final in Lisbon.

1977   Bob Paisley's Liverpool won the European Cup for the first time, beating Borussia Moenchengladbach 3–1 in the final in Rome.

2005   Liverpool won the European Cup for the fifth time, this time in Istanbul, beating AC Milan 3–2 on penalties after a dramatic second-half comeback.

26 May

1938   Arsenal favourites Ted Drake and Cliff Bastin both scored in their last game for England, which ended in a 4–2 victory over France in Paris.

1982   Aston Villa won the European Cup for the first time, beating Bayern Munich for the sixth successive English triumph in the competition.

1987   Left back Nigel Winterburn was signed from Wimbledon. He scored 12 times in 583 games for Arsenal between 1987/88 and 1999/2000, and was capped twice by England.

1989   Arsenal pipped Liverpool to the League title in unforgettably dramatic fashion as Michael Thomas' last-gasp goal clinched a sensational 2–0 win at Anfield.

1999   Manchester United clinched the Treble after a dramatic 2–1 victory over Bayern Munich in the European Cup Final.

27 May

1931   Jack Lambert netted four goals as Herbert Chapman's team gained a 6–1 friendly win over a Swedish XI in Stockholm.

1933   Scottish goalkeeper Alex Wilson was signed from Greenock Morton. He made 82 First Division appearances for the Gunners between 1933 and 1939.

1948   Inside-left Doug Lishman arrived from Walsall. He was a clinical finisher and a brilliant header of the ball who was Arsenal's leading scorer in five campaigns but was passed over for the 1950 FA Cup Final squad.

1953   Dennis Evans made his debut as Cliff Holton scored twice in Arsenal's 2–1 friendly victory over Grasshoppers in Zurich.

1998   Ian Wright was injured during England's 1–0 win over Morocco in Casablanca, ending his hopes of making the final World Cup squad.

28 May

1900   Winger Frank Lloyd moved to Aston Villa. He netted three goals in 18 Second Division outings for the Gunners during the 1899/1900 campaign.

1937   Reg Lewis scored twice on his debut as George Allison's side eased to a 4-1 friendly victory over Copenhagen in Denmark.

1956   England Youth wing-half Johnny Petts signed professional terms for Arsenal. He made 32 appearances for the Gunners between 1957/58 and 1961/62.

1976   Arsenal goalkeeper Jimmy Rimmer made his sole appearance for England in the 3-2 win over Italy in an exhibition match in New York.

1980   Brian Clough's Nottingham Forest retained the European Cup, beating SV Hamburg 1-0 with a goal by John Robertson.

29 May

1931   David Jack netted a hat-trick as Arsenal beat AIK Stockholm 5-0 in the penultimate match of their Scandinavian tour.

1959   Midfielder Steve Gatting was born in Park Royal, London. The brother of England cricket captain Mike Gatting, he scored six times in 76 outings for Arsenal between 1978/79 and 1980/81.

1968   Bobby Charlton scored twice as Manchester United won the European Cup for the first time, beating Benfica 4-1 at Wembley.

1985   The Heysel Stadium disaster left 39 people dead after rioting during the European Cup Final between Liverpool and Juventus.

1990   England Under-21 striker Martin Hayes was sold to Celtic. He netted 34 goals in 132 games for the Gunners between 1985/86 and 1989/90 and ended his professional career at Swansea City.

30 May

1935 Footballing cricketer Jim Standen was born in Edmonton, London. The goal-keeper made 35 First Division appearances for Arsenal.

1951 Substitute Don Roper scored to give the Gunners a 1–0 friendly win over São Paulo in the fourth match of their Brazilian tour.

1952 Arsenal wing-half Alex Forbes made his 14th and last appearance for Scotland in the 3–1 defeat by Sweden in Stockholm.

1964 Joe Baker grabbed a hat-trick as Billy Wright's team swept to a 5–0 friendly victory over a South Africa XI in Johannesburg.

1995 Arsenal's former England international centre forward Ted Drake, 82, died in London. He scored a Club-record 42 League goals in 1934/35.

31 May

1884 England international inside forward Frank Bradshaw was born in Sheffield. He scored 14 times in 132 League games for the Gunners, whom he served from 1914 to 1922.

1941 Two goals by Bobby Beattie gave Preston North End a 2–1 win over Arsenal in the Football League War Cup Final replay.

1947 Strikes by Ronnie Rooke and Reg Lewis earned the Gunners a 2–1 First Division victory over Everton at Highbury.

1960 Centre forward Len Julians joined Nottingham Forest. He netted ten goals in 24 outings for Arsenal during 1958/59 and 1959/60 and went on to play for Millwall before coaching in the United States.

1980 Arsenal striker Alan Sunderland made his sole appearance for England in the 2–1 win over Australia in Sydney.

1 June

1929 Scotland international inside left Alex James joined from Preston North End. He netted 26 goals in 231 League games during his illustrious Arsenal career.

1940 Les Jones scored twice as the Gunners completed their wartime League South C Division games with a 5–0 win at home to Southampton.

1949 Reg Lewis netted twice as Tom Whittaker's Arsenal gained a 2–2 friendly draw against Brazilian team Botafogo in Rio de Janeiro.

1953 Arsenal's former Scotland international inside left Alex James, 51, died in London. He starred in the glory days under Herbert Chapman, helping to win the League title four times and the FA Cup twice.

1955 Winger Ben Marden moved from Arsenal to Watford. After leaving the Hornets he served two non-League clubs, Bedford Town and Romford.

2 June

1934 Tough-tackling England international Wilf Copping joined Arsenal from Leeds United. Dubbed 'The Iron Man', he formed a tremendously effective wing-half partnership with Jack Crayston.

1937 Reg Lewis scored for the third consecutive match as Arsenal gained a 3–0 friendly victory over Copenhagen in Denmark.

1968 Jim Furnell made his final appearance for Arsenal as Dave Jenkins netted a hat-trick in a 6–3 friendly win over the President's XI in Kuala Lumpur.

1991 England Under-21 defender Gus Caesar moved to Cambridge United. He made 50 appearances for Arsenal between 1985/86 and 1990/91.

2002 Sol Campbell, David Seaman and Ashley Cole featured in England's 1–1 World Cup group draw with Sweden in Saitama.

3 June

1931   David Jack, Jack Lambert and Cliff Bastin scored in Arsenal's 3–2 friendly win over Gothenburg Combination in Sweden.

1939   Scottish inside forward Jimmy Logie was signed from Lochore Welfare. He was an inventive performer blessed with delicate ball skills, who offered tremendous service to his fellow attackers.

1970   Striker Bobby Gould was sold to Wolverhampton Wanderers. Later he served West Bromwich Albion and Bristol City among many others.

1988   Central defender Steve Bould arrived at Highbury from Stoke City. He netted eight goals in 371 outings for Arsenal between 1988/89 and 1998/99.

2003   Long-serving England international goalkeeper David Seaman moved to Manchester City. He won 72 caps during his Highbury sojourn.

4 June

1939   Dave Nelson and George Drury netted two goals apiece in Arsenal's 5–1 friendly win over Diables Rouges in Brussels.

1949   Welsh international Bryn Jones made his final appearance for Arsenal as the Gunners lost 1–0 to São Paulo in the last match of their Brazilian tour.

1977   Austrian international goalkeeper Alex Manninger was born in Salzburg. He made 39 appearances for the Gunners between 1997/98 and 2001/02.

1983   Ivory Coast international defender Emmanuel Eboue was born in Abidjan. He joined Arsenal from Beveren on New Year's Day 2005.

1992   Arsenal's long-serving central defender David O'Leary featured in the Republic of Ireland's 2–0 defeat by Italy in Foxboro.

5 June

1903   Arsenal manager Harry Bradshaw signed left back Fred Dwight from Fulham. He played one League game in January 1905 as Jimmy Jackson's understudy.

1991   Striker Kwame Ampadu moved to West Bromwich Albion. He made two First Division appearances for the Gunners.

1993   Arsenal midfielder Ray Parlour helped England Under-21s to beat their Belgian counterparts 2–1 in a tournament in Toulon.

1999   David Seaman, Martin Keown and Ray Parlour featured in England's 0–0 draw with Sweden in the European Championship qualifier at Wembley.

2004   Arsenal defenders Ashley Cole and Sol Campbell helped England hammer Iceland 6–1 at the City of Manchester Stadium in a pre World Cup warm-up game.

6 June

1906   Scottish left-half Archie Low arrived from Glasgow side Ashfield. He made three League appearances for the Gunners.

1930   Ex-England international Jack Butler joined Torquay United. He netted seven goals in 267 League games for Arsenal.

1937   Alex James made his final appearance for Arsenal as Arthur Biggs scored twice in Arsenal's 3–0 friendly win over Feyenoord in Rotterdam.

1951   Jimmy Logie was on target as the Gunners suffered a 3–1 friendly defeat by Brazilian side Palmeiras in São Paulo.

2002   Arsenal trio Thierry Henry, Patrick Vieira and Sylvain Wiltord featured in France's 0–0 World Cup draw against Uruguay in Busan, South Korea.

7 June

1928 Welsh international left-half Dave Bowen was born in Nantyffyllon, Glamorgan. He scored twice in 162 games for the Gunners between 1950/51 and 1958/59.

1947 Colin Collindridge and George Jones scored in Sheffield United's 2–1 First Division win over Arsenal at Bramall Lane.

1948 Winger Alf Morgan moved from Arsenal to Walsall. He made two First Division appearances while at Highbury.

1992 Arsenal central defender David O'Leary helped the Republic of Ireland to defeat Portugal 2–0 in Boston, USA.

2002 Arsenal trio David Seaman, Ashley Cole and Sol Campbell starred in England's 1–0 World Cup win over Argentina in Sapporo, Japan.

8 June

1899 Scottish right back Duncan McNichol was signed from St Bernards. He scored once in 101 League outings for the Gunners between 1899 and 1903.

1905 Scotland international left back Jimmy Sharp, who had earlier thrived north of the border with Dundee, arrived from Fulham.

1914 England international forward Frank Bradshaw was signed from Everton. He bagged a hat-trick on his sole appearance for his country.

1954 England left back Lionel Smith, capped six times, moved to Watford. He made 162 First Division appearances during a Highbury sojourn from 1947/48 to 1953/54.

1982 England international striker Tony Woodcock, capped 42 times, arrived from Cologne. He netted 68 goals in 169 games for Arsenal.

9 June

1928   Arsenal winger John Lee moved to Chesterfield. He helped the Gunners twice win the London Combination title.

1936   Ex-Scotland international Frank Hill was sold to Blackpool. 'Tiger' had featured in three League Championship campaigns and won three caps for his country between 1930 and 1931.

1984   Former Northern Ireland international right back John Mackie, 81, died in Isleworth. He won club and international honours during his Portsmouth days.

1986   Central defender Martin Keown was sold to Aston Villa. The England international later rejoined Arsenal via Everton (see 4 Feb, page 25).

1992   Arsenal right back Lee Dixon and striker Ian Wright featured in England's 2–0 defeat by the United States in Foxboro, Massachusetts.

10 June

1919   Republic of Ireland international Dr Kevin O'Flanagan was born in Dublin. He scored three times in 14 League games for Arsenal in 1946/47.

1946   Inside forward Tommy Baldwin was born in Gateshead. He netted 11 goals in 20 outings while at Highbury from 1964/65 to 1966/67.

1966   England international midfielder David Platt was born in Chadderton, Lancashire. He scored 15 times in 107 games for Arsenal between 1995/96 and 1997/98.

1984   Arsenal pair Kenny Sansom and Tony Woodcock featured prominently as England defeated Brazil 2–0 in Rio de Janeiro.

1985   England international midfielder Brian Talbot, who was capped six times, joined Watford. He starred in Arsenal's 1979 FA Cup Final success.

11 June

1977   Arsenal full backs Pat Rice and Sammy Nelson featured in Northern Ireland's 1–0 World Cup qualifier defeat by Iceland in Reykjavik.

1992   Arsenal pair Paul Merson and Alan Smith took part in England's 0–0 group-stage draw against Denmark in the European Championship.

2000   Arsenal trio Thierry Henry, Emmanuel Petit and Patrick Vieira were prominent in France's 3–0 European Championship win over Denmark.

2000   Dennis Bergkamp and Marc Overmars helped Holland clinch a 1–0 victory over the Czech Republic in the European Championship.

2002   Patrick Vieira and Sylvain Wiltord played as holders France went out of the World Cup with a 2–0 defeat by Denmark in Incheon, South Korea.

12 June

1945   Northern Ireland international goalkeeper Pat Jennings was born in Newry. He made 326 appearances for the Gunners and totalled 119 caps.

1946   Much-travelled striker Bobby Gould was born in Coventry. He excelled with his hometown club before arriving at Highbury, then served six more clubs.

1980   Striker Clive Allen joined Arsenal from QPR. His father Les, brother Bradley and nephew Martin also played for Rangers. Clive never played a senior game for the Gunners, but moved to Crystal Palace, then served several more clubs, notably Tottenham Hotspur.

1983   Alan Sunderland, Raphael Meade, Lee Chapman, Brian McDermott and Kenny Sansom all scored in Arsenal's 5–0 friendly win over VSPSSI in Djakarta, Indonesia.

1998   Arsenal midfielder Emmanuel Petit played for host nation France in their 3–0 win over South Africa in Group C in the World Cup finals.

13 June

1955   Arsenal wing-half Arthur Shaw moved to Watford. He featured in the Gunners'
1952/53 League Championship success.

1983   Republic of Ireland international John Devine joined Norwich City. He made 89
First Division appearances for the Gunners.

1992   Arsenal players Ian Wright and Paul Merson appeared for England in the 1–1
draw against Brazil in Washington, USA.

1998   Arsenal pair Marc Overmars and Dennis Bergkamp featured in Holland's 0–0
draw with Belgium in Group E in the World Cup finals.

2004   Patrick Vieira, Thierry Henry, Robert Pires and Sylvain Wiltord helped France
beat England 2–1 in the European Championship.

14 June

1973   Hard-tackling Arsenal midfielder Peter Storey won his 19th and last cap for
England in the 2–0 defeat by Italy in Turin.

1973   Central defender David O'Leary joined Arsenal as an apprentice. He went on to
make 719 senior appearances for the Club, more than any other Gunner.

1974   England Under-21 midfielder Ian Selley was born in Chertsey, Surrey. He made
60 appearances while at Highbury and scored 2 goals between 1992/93 and
1996/97.

1990   England Under-21 goalkeeper John Lukic returned to Leeds United. He played
297 games for the Gunners from 1983/84 to 1989/90 and 1996/97 to
2000/01, featuring in the Club's 1988/89 League Championship campaign.

2001   England Under-21 striker Francis Jeffers arrived from Everton. He gained full
international recognition while at Highbury before moving to Charlton Athletic.

15 June

1912   England Test cricketer and Arsenal centre-forward cum wing-half Andy Ducat was sold to Aston Villa. He scored 19 times in 187 League games for the Gunners between 1904/05 and 1911/12.

1935   Winger Jackie Milne was signed from Blackburn Rovers. He won full and wartime international honours with Middlesbrough.

1935   Derbyshire cricketer and Arsenal inside-forward Ray Swallow was born in Southwark, London. He netted four goals in 13 games for Arsenal.

1974   Midfielder Trevor Ross signed professional for Arsenal. He gained Scotland Under-21 recognition while at Highbury and played 67 games and scored 9 goals for the Gunners between 1974/75 and 1977/78.

1998   Arsenal pair David Seaman and Tony Adams featured in England's 2–0 win over Tunisia in Group G in the World Cup finals.

16 June

1982   Graham Rix and Kenny Sansom played for England in the World Cup finals in Spain, helping to beat France 3–1.

1983   Arsenal rounded off their tour of Indonesia as Terry Neill's side lost 2–0 to VSNIAC Mitra in a friendly in Surabaja.

1985   Arsenal full backs Viv Anderson and Kenny Sansom featured in England's 5–0 victory over the United States in Los Angeles.

1994   Goalkeeper Lee Harper was signed from Sittingbourne. He made one Premiership appearance when David Seaman and John Lukic were unavailable.

2000   Cameroon international Lauren arrived from Real Mallorca. He helped his country win the African Nations Cup and Olympics that year.

17 June

1895   Long-serving inside forward Billy Blyth was born in Dalkeith, Midlothian. He captained Arsenal in the 1927 FA Cup Final, which was lost to Cardiff City (see 23 April, page 64).

1919   Winger Tommy Rudkin was born in Worksop, Nottinghamshire. He scored twice in five First Division appearances for the Gunners.

1952   Winger Gerry Ward joined Arsenal as an amateur. He netted ten goals in 81 First Division games while at Highbury between 1953/54 and 1962/63.

1953   Welsh international centre half Ray Daniel joined Sunderland. He scored five times in 87 League games for Arsenal.

2000   Arsenal pair David Seaman and Martin Keown featured in England's 1–0 victory over Germany in the European Championship at Charleroi, Belgium.

18 June

1914   Wing-half George Jobey moved to Bradford Park Avenue. He scored three times in 28 League outings for the Gunners.

1962   England B international central defender Andy Linighan was born in Hartlepool, County Durham. He netted eight goals in 155 games for Arsenal, famously scoring in the 1993 FA Cup Final replay (see 20 May, page 78).

1979   Midfielder Paul Davis signed as a professional for Arsenal. He scored 37 times in 445 outings between 1979/80 and 1994/95.

1993   Republic of Ireland international Eddie McGoldrick was signed from Crystal Palace. He was transferred to Manchester City in 1996.

2004   Arsenal midfielder Freddie Ljungberg helped Sweden draw 1–1 with Italy in Oporto, Portugal, in the European Championship.

19 June

1913 Footballing cricketer Wally Hardinge, who played once for England at both sports, arrived at Highbury from Sheffield United. He netted 14 goals in 54 League games for the Gunners.

1933 Centre forward Len Julians was born in Tottenham. He started his career with Leyton Orient before becoming a Gunner.

1944 Arsenal's England international centre half Herbie Roberts, 39, died from a skin disease. He was renowned as one of the first 'stoppers' at the heart of a defence.

1993 Arsenal players Martin Keown, Paul Merson, Nigel Winterburn and Ian Wright featured in England's 2–1 friendly defeat by Germany in Detroit.

2001 Dutch international Giovanni van Bronckhorst arrived from Glasgow Rangers. He took part in the 2001/02 Premiership title campaign.

20 June

1949 Free-scoring centre forward Ronnie Rooke became Crystal Palace's player-manager. He netted 68 goals in 88 League games for Arsenal after arriving from Fulham in 1946.

1984 Midfielder Dave Madden joined Charlton Athletic. He helped Arsenal to win the Football Combination title in 1983/84.

1987 Winger Ian Allinson moved from Arsenal to Stoke City. He scored 16 times in 83 First Division outings for the Gunners.

1989 Goalkeeper Andy Marriott joined Nottingham Forest. He failed to make a first-team appearance for Arsenal but became a Welsh international.

1998 Arsenal pair Marc Overmars and Dennis Bergkamp scored in Holland's 5–0 win over South Korea in Group E in the World Cup finals in Marseilles, France.

21 June

1951   England international midfielder Alan Hudson, who was capped twice, was born in Chelsea. He made 36 First Division appearances while at Highbury during 1976/77 and 1977/78.

1982   Arsenal goalkeeper Pat Jennings featured prominently in Northern Ireland's 1–1 World Cup draw with Honduras.

2002   Arsenal trio David Seaman, Ashley Cole and Sol Campbell played in England's 2–1 defeat by Brazil in the World Cup quarter-finals.

2004   Gunners Ashley Cole and Sol Campbell helped England beat Croatia 4–2 and qualify for the European Championship quarter-finals.

2004   Thierry Henry scored twice as France defeated Switzerland 3–1 to finish top of Group B in the European Championship.

22 June

1900   Right half Fred Coles was signed from Nottingham Forest. He scored twice in 78 League outings for the Gunners.

1904   Right half Jim Bigden arrived from West Ham United. He netted once in 75 First Division games for Arsenal.

1983   Scotland international striker Charlie Nicholas joined Arsenal from Celtic. He had plundered more than half a century of goals in his last season north of the border.

1988   England international midfielder Graham Rix, who won 17 caps, joined French side Caen. He netted 51 goals in 463 games for Arsenal between 1976/77 and 1987/88.

1998   Arsenal pair David Seaman and Tony Adams played in England's 2–1 defeat by Romania in Group G in the World Cup finals played in Toulouse, France.

23 June

1955 England Youth midfielder David Price was born in Caterham, Surrey. He scored 19 times in 175 games while at Highbury from 1972/73 to 1980/81.

1971 Former Arsenal and England Under-23 international inside forward Jimmy Bloomfield replaced Frank O'Farrell as Leicester City's manager

1976 French international midfielder Patrick Vieira was born in Dakar, Senegal. He netted 28 goals in 279 Premiership games for Arsenal during a fabulous Highbury career which stretched from 1996/97 to 2004/05.

1976 Former Arsenal and Northern Ireland centre-half Terry Neill resigned after two years as manager of local rivals Tottenham Hotspur.

2000 England international left-back Nigel Winterburn joined West Ham United. He had served Wimbledon for four seasons before setting out on his long and illustrious Highbury sojourn.

24 June

1949 Former Welsh international Bryn Jones joined Norwich City as player-coach. He scored seven times in 71 League games for Arsenal.

1962 Left-back Brian Sparrow was born in London. He helped Arsenal win the Football Combination title in 1983/84, making two appearances for the Club.

1987 Italian Youth striker Arturo Lupoli was born in Brescia. He featured in Arsenal's 2004/05 Carling Cup run, scoring twice in three games.

1998 Arsenal midfielders Emmanuel Petit and Patrick Vieira played in France's 2–1 victory over Denmark in Group C in the World Cup finals played in Lyon, France.

2004 Sol Campbell was unfortunate to have an effort disallowed as England drew 2–2 with Portugal, then lost 6–5 on penalties in the European Championship.

25 June

1904 Right half Fred Coles moved from Woolwich Arsenal to Grimsby Town. Later he became a football and cricket coach in Gothenburg, Sweden.

1982 Arsenal goalkeeper Pat Jennings starred in Northern Ireland's surprising 1–0 World Cup win over host nation Spain. The Ulstermen finished top of Group 5.

1992 England international winger Chris Waddle returned from French club Marseilles to join Sheffield Wednesday.

1997 French international midfielder Emmanuel Petit was signed from Monaco. He was reunited with his former manager Arsène Wenger at Highbury.

2004 Thierry Henry, Robert Pires and Sylvain Wiltord featured as holders France lost 1–0 to Greece in the European Championship quarter-finals.

26 June

1939 Welsh winger Wilf Walsh moved from Arsenal to Derby County. He made three First Division appearances for the Gunners.

1970 Northern Ireland international Terry Neill joined Hull City as player-manager. Later in his career he managed Tottenham Hotspur, then took over the Highbury reins from 1976 to 1983.

1972 Striker Frank Stapleton joined Arsenal as an apprentice. He netted 108 goals in 299 outings while at Highbury between 1974/75 and 1980/81 and featured in the Club's 1978/79 FA Cup campaign.

1987 Much-travelled former Arsenal striker Bobby Gould left Bristol Rovers to succeed Dave Bassett as manager of Wimbledon.

1998 Arsenal duo David Seaman and Tony Adams played in England's 2–0 win over Colombia in Group G in the World Cup finals played in Lens, France.

27 June

1972 Ex-England international striker Geoff Hurst, who scored a hat-trick in the 1966 World Cup final, moved from West Ham to Stoke City.

1978 Midfielder Paul Davis joined Arsenal as an apprentice. He featured in two League Championship successes while at Highbury, in 1988/89 and 1990/91.

1997 England international striker Teddy Sheringham moved from Tottenham Hotspur to Manchester United.

1999 Brazilian international full back Silvinho was signed from Corinthians. He scored three times in 55 Premiership games for Arsenal.

2005 Belarus international midfielder Alexander Hleb joined Arsenal from Stuttgart. He was his country's Sportsperson of the Year.

28 June

1913 England international goalkeeper Joe Lievesley arrived from Sheffield United. He made 73 League appearances for the Gunners.

1923 Centre forward Harry Woods was signed from Newcastle United. He netted 21 goals in 70 First Division games for Arsenal.

1928 Northern Ireland international full back John Mackie was sold to Portsmouth. His sole cap was awarded in 1923.

1929 England Amateur international full back Stan Charlton was born in Exeter, Devon. He played 99 First Division games while at Highbury.

1998 Arsenal midfielder Emmanuel Petit helped France to overcome Paraguay with a 'golden goal' in extra time in the World Cup finals.

29 June

1923   Twice-capped England international goalkeeper Ernie Williamson moved to Norwich City after 105 League appearances for Arsenal between 1919 and 1922.

1950   Larry Gaertjens scored to give the United States a shock 1–0 World Cup victory over England in Belo Horizonte, Brazil.

1982   Arsenal players Kenny Sansom and Graham Rix were in the England side which drew 0–0 against West Germany in the World Cup.

1998   Arsenal pair Dennis Bergkamp, who scored, and Marc Overmars featured in Holland's 2–1 World Cup victory over Yugoslavia in Toulouse, France.

2003   Arsenal striker Thierry Henry's 97th-minute golden goal clinched France's victory over Cameroon in the Confederations Cup Final in Paris.

30 June

1914   Centre forward Steve Stonley moved from Arsenal to Brentford. He scored 14 times in 38 League games for the Gunners.

1932   Welsh international inside forward Derek Tapscott, who was capped 14 times between 1954 and 1959, was born in Barry. He netted 68 goals in 132 outings for Arsenal, being based at Highbury from 1953/54 to 1957/58.

1975   Goalkeeper Rami Shaaban was born in Stockholm. He made three Premiership appearances as David Seaman's understudy during 2002/03 and 2003/04.

1995   England Under-21 striker Kevin Campbell joined Nottingham Forest. He scored 59 times in 226 games for Arsenal between 1987/88 and 1994/95 and went on to play for Turkish team Trabzonspor before ending his professional days at Everton.

1998   Gunners David Seaman and Tony Adams were in action as England lost 4–3 on penalties after a 2–2 draw with Argentina in the World Cup at St. Etienne.

1 July

1961   Scotland international winger Johnny MacLeod arrived from Hibernian. He netted 28 goals in 112 games for Arsenal before moving to Aston Villa in 1964.

1966   Northern Ireland international Billy McCullough moved to Millwall. He scored five times in 268 outings while at Highbury between 1958/59 and 1965/66.

1977   Defender Kevin Stead followed Terry Neill from Tottenham Hotspur to Arsenal. He made two appearances for the Gunners during 1977/78.

1987   England international right back Viv Anderson moved from Arsenal to Manchester United. He had scored 15 goals in 150 games for the Gunners.

1990   Midfielder Kevin Richardson joined Real Sociedad. Unobtrusively excellent, he netted five goals in 96 First Division games for Arsenal.

2 July

1970   Northern Ireland international Steve Morrow was born in Belfast. After his Highbury days, between 1991/92 and 1996/97, he moved to QPR, where he served under former Arsenal assistant boss Stewart Houston.

1975   Striker Charlie George was sold to Derby County. He netted 31 goals in 133 First Division outings for Arsenal in a memorable Highbury sojourn from 1969/70 to 1974/75.

1977   Goalkeeper Bob Wilson re-signed for Arsenal as emergency cover but stayed with the BBC as linkman and commentator.

1986   England international striker Gary Lineker moved from Everton to Terry Venables' Barcelona in a record £4,261,000 deal.

1990   The FA reduced Swindon Town's punishment after an illegal-payments scandal and allowed them to stay in the Second Division.

3 July

1925   Six-times capped England international Charlie Buchan joined Arsenal from Sunderland for £2,000 plus £100 for each goal he scored for the Gunners.

1966   Arsenal inside forward George Eastham scored in his 19th and last appearance for England in the 2–0 win over Denmark in Copenhagen after winning 19 caps.

1995   Dutch international striker Dennis Bergkamp was recruited from Inter Milan. He was Bruce Rioch's first signing as Arsenal manager.

2000   French international striker Robert Pires arrived from Marseilles. He helped his country win the European Championship later that summer.

2001   Arsène Wenger signed England international central defender Sol Campbell from local rivals Tottenham Hotspur.

4 July

1974   Former Leeds United boss Don Revie was appointed new England team manager in succession to Sir Alf Ramsey.

1982   Arsenal goalkeeper Pat Jennings featured as Northern Ireland were knocked out of the World Cup in the second round, losing 4–1 to France.

1990   England lost 4–3 on penalties after a 1–1 draw with eventual winners West Germany in the World Cup semi-final in Turin.

1990   Central defender Andy Linighan arrived from Norwich City. He netted eight goals in 155 games for Arsenal, famously scoring the 1993 FA Cup Final replay against Sheffield Wednesday (see 20 May, page 78).

1998   Dennis Bergkamp broke Holland's goalscoring record with a stunning winner against Argentina in the World Cup quarter-finals in Marseilles, France.

5 July

1972 Arsenal midfielder George Graham was in the Scotland team defeated 1–0 by Brazil in Rio de Janeiro with a late goal from Jairzinho.

1975 Republic of Ireland international Johnny Giles left Leeds United to replace Don Howe as West Bromwich Albion's player-boss.

1978 Goalkeeper Paul Barron was signed from Plymouth Argyle. He played eight First Division games for the Gunners during 1978/79 and 1979/80.

1990 Chelsea signed midfielders Andy Townsend from Norwich City for £1,200,000 and Dennis Wise from Wimbledon for £1,600,000.

2001 England international goalkeeper Richard Wright arrived from Ipswich Town. He made 12 Premiership appearances for Arsenal, then went on to serve Everton.

6 July

1959 Welsh international Dave Bowen rejoined Northampton Town as player-manager. He engineered the Cobblers' meteoric rise to the top-flight.

1979 West Bromwich Albion coach Colin Addison succeeded another former Arsenal player, Tommy Docherty, as Derby County's manager.

1988 England Under-21 midfielder Paul Gascoigne moved from Newcastle United to Tottenham Hotspur in a record £2,000,000 deal.

1995 Winger Jimmy Carter moved from Arsenal to Portsmouth. He scored twice in 29 outings while at Highbury from 1991/92 to 1994/95 and had an injury time goal disallowed during Arsenal's 2–1 FA Cup defeat by Wrexham.

1998 Ex-Northern Ireland international Danny Wilson returned to Sheffield Wednesday as manager, with John Hendrie succeeding him at Barnsley.

7 July

1921   Long-serving left back Joe Wade was born in Shoreditch, London. He made 86 First Division appearances during a Highbury sojourn from 1944/45 to 1955/56.

1982   Bobby Robson, who had worked wonders during 13 years in charge of Ipswich Town, was appointed England manager.

1997   England international striker Paul Merson, capped 21 times, moved to Middlesbrough. He netted 99 goals in 422 outings for the Gunners between 1986/87 and 1996/97.

1998   Former England international captain David Platt, 32, announced his retirement with a year still to run on his Arsenal contract.

1998   Dennis Bergkamp featured as Holland were beaten 4–2 on penalties after a 1–1 draw against Brazil in the World Cup semi-finals played in Marseilles, France.

8 July

1977   Ex-England Schoolboy international Wilf Rostron left Arsenal for Sunderland. He scored twice in 19 outings for the Gunners from 1974/75 to 1976/77.

1990   Swedish international winger Anders Limpar arrived from Cremonese in Italy. He netted 20 goals in 115 games for Arsenal between 1990/91 and 1993/94 before moving to Everton.

1998   Arsenal duo Emmanuel Petit and Thierry Henry helped host nation France reach the World Cup Final with a 2–1 victory over Croatia in Saint-Denis.

1999   French Under-21 striker Kaba Diawara moved to Marseilles. He made 12 Premiership appearances during his spell at Highbury.

2002   Arsène Wenger signed French central defender Pascal Cygan from Lille. He took part in Arsenal's 2003/04 Premiership title triumph.

9 July

1910   Inside forward Willis Rippon was signed from First Division rivals Bristol City. He scored twice in nine League outings for the Gunners.

1971   Arsenal coach Don Howe returned to West Bromwich Albion as manager. He had coached the Gunners to their 1970/71 Double success.

1976   Former Arsenal captain Terry Neill rejoined the Gunners as manager after spells in charge of Hull City and Tottenham Hotspur.

1999   Ukraine international full back Oleg Luzhny arrived from Dynamo Kiev. He featured in Arsenal's 2003 FA Cup Final victory over Southampton and played 109 games for Arsenal between 1999/2000 and 2002/03.

2004   Republic of Ireland Under-21 goalkeeper Graham Stack joined Millwall on a season-long loan. He helped Arsenal win the FA Youth Cup in 2000.

10 July

1920   Centre forward Cyril Grant was born in Wath upon Dearne, Yorkshire. He made two First Division appearances while at Highbury.

1956   Republic of Ireland international striker Frank Stapleton was born in Dublin. He played for Arsenal in three successive FA Cup Finals, in 1978, 1979 and 1980.

1975   England international left back Bob McNab joined Wolverhampton Wanderers. He scored six times in 365 games for Arsenal between 1966/67 and 1974/75 and went on to play in the United States and coach in Canada.

1978   Tottenham Hotspur signed Argentinian World Cup stars Ossie Ardiles and Ricky Villa on their return to the First Division.

1998   Ace marksman Ian Wright was absent as the Double winners started their pre-season fixtures with a 5–2 victory at Boreham Wood.

11 July

1890 Scotland international centre half Alex Graham, capped once in 1921, was born in Hurlford, Ayrshire. He netted 17 goals in 166 League outings for the Gunners between 1912/13 and 1923/24.

1922 Scottish left-half Angus McKinnon moved to Charlton Athletic. He scored four times in 211 League games for the Gunners.

1956 Goalkeeper Ralph Guthrie joined hometown Hartlepool United. He made two First Division appearances while at Highbury.

1998 Arsenal's Dennis Bergkamp and Marc Overmars were in action as Holland lost 2–1 to Croatia in the World Cup third-place play-off in Paris.

2000 Arsenal's new signing, Brazilian-born central midfielder Edu, arrived from Sao Paulo club Corinthians.

12 July

1958 England international midfielder Steve Williams, who won six caps, was born in Hammersmith, London. He netted five goals in 121 outings for Arsenal.

1963 England amateur international Gerry Ward joined Leyton Orient. A skilled passer and tackler, he could play as a wing half or an inside forward.

1974 England international Ray Kennedy, who played 17 times for his country, was sold to Liverpool. He netted 71 goals in 212 games while at Highbury between 1969/70 and 1973/74.

1974 Twice-capped England international striker Brian Kidd arrived at Arsenal from Manchester United. He went on to score 34 goals in 90 games for the Club.

1998 World champion Gunners' midfielders Patrick Vieira and Emmanuel Petit helped host nation France to beat Brazil 3–0 in the World Cup Final at Saint-Denis.

13 July

1970   Midfielder David Court was sold to Luton Town. He scored 17 times in 175 First Division outings for Arsenal between 1962/63 and 1969/70.

1971   Arsenal's reserve-team coach Steve Burtenshaw was appointed first-team coach at Highbury in succession to Don Howe.

1987   England international striker Peter Beardsley moved from Newcastle United to Liverpool in a £1,900,000 deal.

1998   England striker Ian Wright, capped 33 times in the 1990s, joined West Ham United. He remains Arsenal's highest League cup scorer. In the twilight of his dazzling career he did stints with Nottingham Forest on loan, Celtic and Burnley.

2000   England Youth striker Jay Bothroyd moved to Coventry City. He gained England Under-21 honours while at Highfield Road.

14 July

1947   Scotland international wing-half Archie Macaulay joined from Brentford. He scored once in 103 League outings during his stint at Highbury.

1976   Assistant-manager Wilf Dixon left rivals Tottenham Hotspur to team up once again with Terry Neill at Highbury.

1989   Ex-Welsh Youth goalkeeper Rhys Wilmot joined Plymouth Argyle. He made eight First Division appearances for Arsenal.

1995   England international captain David Platt, capped 62 times, arrived from Sampdoria. He went on to contribute significantly to Arsenal's 1997/98 Double success.

1999   German midfielder Stefan Malz was signed from TSV Munich. He scored once in six Premiership games for the Gunners.

15 July

1946   Centre forward Cyril Grant was signed from Lincoln City, mainly as cover for top scorer Reg Lewis and he never claimed a regular first-team berth.

1953   Winger Freddie Cox moved to West Bromwich Albion as player-coach. He scored nine goals in 79 League outings for the Gunners between 1949/50 and 1952/53.

1979   England international midfielder John Hollins, capped once as a Chelsea player, joined from QPR. He was Arsenal's Player of the Year in 1981/82.

1995   Midfielder Stephen Hughes signed as a professional for Arsenal. The England Under-21 international later served Everton, Watford, Charlton Athletic and Coventry City.

2002   Arsenal manager Arsène Wenger was made a member of the Légion d'Honneur in Paris after the Club's outstanding 2001/02 Double success.

16 July

1946   John Hollins was born in Guildford, Surrey. He scored nine times in 127 First Division games for Arsenal between 1979/80 and 1982/83.

1954   Inside forward Jimmy Bloomfield arrived from Brentford. After retiring as a player he managed Orient (twice) and Leicester City.

1962   England centre forward Joe Baker joined from Torino of Italy. After leaving Arsenal he scored goals for Nottingham Forest, Sunderland, Hibernian and Raith Rovers.

1963   Goalkeeper Bob Wilson, capped twice by Scotland, was signed from Wolverhampton Wanderers.

1977   Malcolm Macdonald grabbed a hat-trick as Arsenal gained a 5–1 friendly win over Singapore in the second match of their tour.

17 July

1897 Goalkeeper Roger Ord was signed from non-League side Hebburn Argyle. He made 89 League appearances for the Gunners.

1903 Samson Haden was born in Royston, near Barnsley. He scored ten times in 88 First Division outings while at Highbury.

1940 England international centre forward Joe Baker was born in Liverpool. He was Arsenal's leading marksman in four successive seasons, from 1962/63 to 1965/66.

1965 Arsenal's Welsh international goalkeeper Dan Lewis, 62, died in Scarborough. He played for the Gunners in the 1927 FA Cup Final.

1991 Alan Smith scored twice as Arsenal began their Swedish tour with a 4–1 friendly win over Stockholm Select in Malarvik.

18 July

1984 Arsenal's England international centre half Bernard Joy, 72, died in Kenton. He starred in the 1937/38 League title success and wrote one of the first histories of Arsenal Football Club, *Forward Arsenal*, in 1952.

1986 Death of Sir Stanley Rous, 91, the grand old man of British football. The great reformer was an honorary life president of FIFA.

1987 George Graham, who had managed Arsenal to Littlewoods Cup success the previous season, was given a new five-year contract.

2000 England international striker Nick Barmby moved from Everton to Liverpool, the first sale to their local rivals in 40 years.

2003 Swiss international central defender Philippe Senderos arrived from Servette. He was part of Arsenal's 2005 FA Cup Final triumph.

19 July

1954   Irish winger Joe Haverty was signed from St Patrick's Athletic. When his Highbury days were done he assisted Blackburn Rovers, Millwall and Bristol Rovers.

1974   Former England Under-23 striker Bryan 'Pop' Robson moved from West Ham United to Sunderland in a club record £145,000 deal.

1993   Republic of Ireland international midfielder Roy Keane moved from Nottingham Forest to Manchester United for £3,750,000.

1995   Arsenal's England international striker Alan Smith, having failed to recover from a long-term knee injury, announced his retirement after eight seasons as a Gunner.

2004   Arsène Wenger signed Spanish goalkeeper Manuel Almunia from Spain's Celta Vigo as deputy to Jens Lehmann.

20 July

1943   England international left back Bob McNab was born in Huddersfield. He was a key figure in Arsenal's 1970/71 Double triumph.

1977   George Armstrong scored Arsenal's goal as Terry Neill's side were defeated 3–1 by an Australia XI in a friendly in Sydney.

1998   UEFA gave Arsenal the go ahead for the following season's UEFA Champions League matches to be staged at Wembley Stadium.

2003   French Under-21 left back Gael Glichy was signed from Cannes. He featured promisingly in Arsenal's 2003/04 Premiership title campaign.

2004   England international Martin Keown, who was capped 43 times, joined Leicester City. He featured in three Premiership title triumphs with the Gunners.

21 July

1898 Tom Whittaker was born in Aldershot. He gave Arsenal tremendous service over 37 years as a player, trainer and then manager from 1919 to 1956.

1953 England midfielder Brian Talbot was born in Ipswich. He served his home-town club dynamically for half a decade before being recruited for Arsenal by Terry Neill.

1987 Alan Smith scored on his debut as the Gunners won 6–0 away to Gloucester City in a testimonial for former Arsenal midfielder Barrie Vassallo.

2000 Arsenal midfielders Tommy Black and Julian Gray joined Crystal Palace. Gray made one appearance for the Gunners while Black played two games.

2005 French international midfielder Patrick Vieira moved to Juventus. He gained a Club-record 79 caps and featured in two League Championship campaigns.

22 July

1934 England international winger Danny Clapton, capped once in 1958, was born in Stepney, London. He netted 27 goals in 225 games for Arsenal between 1954/55 and 1961/62.

1966 Goalkeeper Tony Burns moved from Arsenal to Brighton. He made 31 First Division appearances for the Gunners.

1971 England Under-23 midfielder Jon Sammels joined Leicester City. He scored 52 times in 270 outings for Arsenal between 1962/63 and 1970/71.

1992 England midfielder David Rocastle moved to Leeds United. He went on to play for Manchester City and Chelsea before his tragically premature death.

2004 England midfielder Ray Parlour, capped ten times, joined Middlesbrough. He helped Arsenal win all three major domestic honours.

23 July

1945   Midfield creator Jon Sammels was born in Ipswich. He was a member of the Arsenal squad which lifted the Double in 1970/71.

1956   Northern Ireland international wing-half Bill Dickson joined Mansfield Town. He scored once in 29 League outings for the Gunners.

1984   England international right back Viv Anderson, who was capped 30 times, arrived from Nottingham Forest. He scored 15 times in 150 games for Arsenal during his Highbury stint from 1984/85 to 1986/87.

1988   Steve Bould made his debut as the Gunners triumphed 5–0 away to Yeovil Town in a testimonial for former Arsenal winger Alan Skirton.

2001   Midfielder Junichi Inamoto became the first Japanese signing in English football when he joined Arsenal from Gamba Osaka.

24 July

1870   Goalkeeper Harry Storer was born in Ripley, Derbyshire. He played 40 League games for the Gunners and went on to manage Derby County.

1966   England international central defender Martin Keown was born in Oxford. He netted eight goals in 445 games during two spells at Arsenal during 1985/86 and from 1992/93 to 2003/04.

1991   Joint player-managers Alan Curbishley and Steve Gritt replaced Lennie Lawrence in charge of Charlton Athletic.

2002   England international goalkeeper Richard Wright moved to Everton after playing in Arsenal's 2001/02 Double campaign.

2003   Ukraine international full back Oleg Luzhny joined Wolverhampton Wanderers. He made 109 appearances for Arsenal between 1999/2000 and 2002/03.

25 July

1983   Goalkeeper John Lukic was signed from Leeds United. He played for Arsenal in two consecutive Littlewoods Cup Finals in 1987 and 1988 and featured in the 1998/99 League Championship.

1987   Nigel Winterburn made his debut as Perry Groves' strike clinched Arsenal's 1–0 friendly victory over Morton at Cappielow Park in Greenock, Scotland.

1988   England international midfielder Steve Williams joined Luton Town. The former Southampton star went on to complete his League career with Exeter City.

1998   French Youth defender David Grondin was signed from St Etienne. He made one Premiership appearance for the Gunners.

2003   German international goalkeeper Jens Lehmann arrived from Borussia Dortmund. He was ever-present for Arsenal in 2003/04 and Arsenal didn't lose a League game with him in goal from August 2003 to December 2005.

26 July

1920   Winger Ian McPherson was born in Glasgow. He scored 19 times in 152 First Division outings during his stint at Highbury from 1946 to 1951.

1947   Winger Alf Calverley moved to First Division rivals Preston North End. He made 11 League appearances for Arsenal.

1950   Tom Whittaker paid £1,000 to Northampton Town for left-half Dave Bowen. He proved an able replacement for Joe Mercer as captain of the Gunners.

1961   Scotland international forward David Herd joined Manchester United. He scored twice as the Red Devils beat Leicester City to win the FA Cup in 1963.

1973   Scotland Under-23 winger Peter Marinello was sold to Portsmouth. Later he served Motherwell, Fulham and Heart of Midlothian.

27 July

1913 England international winger Pat Beasley was born in Stourbridge. He played 89 games for Arsenal and went on to manage Bristol City.

1935 Northern Ireland international Billy McCullough was born in Woodburn. The rugged full back was nicknamed 'Flint' after a TV cowboy character of the 1960s.

1968 Dave Jenkins scored twice as Bertie Mee's side suffered a 3–2 friendly defeat against Alemmania Aachen in West Germany.

2000 Republic of Ireland Under-21 central defender Brian McGovern joined Norwich City on loan, signing permanently a month later.

2002 Rioting fans from two local clubs forced Arsenal's friendly against Rapid Vienna in Austria to be abandoned after 67 minutes.

28 July

1901 Half-back Bill Seddon was born in Clapton, London. He helped Arsenal to win the FA Cup in 1930, and was equally at home in the centre or right half.

1951 England international Ray Kennedy was born in Seaton Delaval, Northumberland. He excelled as a striker in the 1970/71 Double campaign, then later starred in midfield for Liverpool.

1989 Icelandic international midfielder Siggi Jonsson joined the Gunners from Sheffield Wednesday. He scored once in nine games for Arsenal.

2000 Marc Overmars and Emmanuel Petit moved to Barcelona in a joint deal. The pair had starred in Arsenal's 1997/98 Double success, and both played more than a century of games for the Gunners.

2002 Brazilian World Cup-winner Gilberto Silva arrived from Atletico Mineiro. He helped Arsenal to lift the Premiership title in 2003/04.

29 July

1912 Scottish winger David Neave moved to Merthyr Town. He netted 30 goals in 154 League games during two spells with the Gunners.

1972 Charlie George and Ray Kennedy scored two goals apiece as Arsenal began their Swiss tour with a 6–0 victory over Lausanne.

1976 England international striker Malcolm Macdonald, who won 14 caps, arrived from Newcastle United. He was Terry Neill's first major signing for Arsenal.

1979 Malcolm Macdonald announced his early retirement due to an arthritic knee. He scored 57 times in 108 games for the Gunners since joining in 1976.

2004 Nigerian international striker Kanu joined West Bromwich Albion. He netted 30 goals in 119 Premiership games for Arsenal between 1998/99 and 2003/04 including a famous 15-minute hat-trick against Chelsea at Stamford Bridge.

30 July

1923 Arsenal left back Arthur Hutchins moved to Charlton Athletic. He scored once in 104 First Division outings while at Highbury.

1966 England won the World Cup, beating West Germany 4–2 after extra time in the Wembley final, with Geoff Hurst scoring a hat-trick.

1969 Strikes by John Radford and Charlie George gave the Gunners a 2–2 friendly draw against Kaiserslautern in West Germany.

1989 Steve Bould's goal clinched Arsenal's 1–0 win over Liverpool in the final of the Makita International Tournament at Wembley.

1991 Alan Smith and Lee Dixon netted in Arsenal's 2–2 draw against Celtic in Paul Davis' testimonial match at Highbury.

31 July

1951   Winger Ian McPherson moved from Arsenal to Notts County. He had started his career with Glasgow Rangers and later served Brentford and non-League Bedford Town.

1961   Republic of Ireland international Joe Haverty joined Blackburn Rovers. He was a tiny flankman but he packed a surprisingly fierce shot.

1970   Charlie George and Jon Sammels netted two goals each as Arsenal gained a 5–0 friendly win over Kungsbacka in Sweden.

1981   Defender Colin Hill signed professional for Arsenal. He scored once in 46 First Division outings while at Highbury.

1983   Charlie Nicholas scored twice on his debut as the Gunners beat Meppen 4–1 in a friendly at the start of their tour of West Germany.

1 August

1956   Scottish international wing-half Alex Forbes moved to Leyton Orient. As a teenager the dynamic redhead played ice hockey for Dundee Tigers and Scotland.

1976   Nigerian international striker Kanu was born in Owerri. He helped Dutch club Ajax to win the European Cup in 1995, then led his country to Olympic gold a year later.

1977   Defender Steve Walford followed Terry Neill from Tottenham Hotspur. He featured in Arsenal's 1979 FA Cup Final triumph and remained a Gunner until 1981.

1980   Republic of Ireland midfield maestro Liam Brady joined Juventus. 'Chippy' later returned to Highbury and took charge of the youth system.

1999   Arsenal came from behind to beat Manchester United 2–1 in the FA Charity Shield at Wembley with second-half goals from Kanu and Ray Parlour.

2 August

1951   Arsenal goalkeeper George Swindin took nine wickets as the Gunners defeated Northern Polytechnic in a cricket match.

1972   Charlie George netted twice as the Gunners gained a 2–1 friendly victory over Swiss side Grasshoppers in Zurich.

1985   Strikes by Stewart Robson and Paul Mariner gave Arsenal a 2–1 friendly win over Brighton and Hove Albion at the Goldstone Ground.

1994   European Cup Winners' Cup holders Arsenal stormed to a 5–1 friendly victory over Stromsgodset in Norway.

1999   French international Nicolas Anelka joined Real Madrid as Croatian star Davor Suker moved in the opposite direction.

3 August

1965   George Eastham, Joe Baker and Jon Sammels netted as Billy Wright's team defeated Trinidad XI 3–1 in a friendly match.

1979   FA Cup holders Arsenal lost 4–3 on penalties after a 0–0 draw against Ajax in the Amsterdam Tournament in Holland.

1991   David Rocastle's strike clinched Arsenal's 1–0 win over Panathinaikos in the Makita International Tournament at Highbury.

1998   Scotland Under-21 central defender Scott Marshall joined Southampton. He scored once in 26 games for Arsenal from 1992/93 to 1997/98.

1999   French international striker Thierry Henry was signed from Juventus, for whom he had scored three times in 16 League appearances. He had helped his country win the World Cup in 1998 and Euro 2000 and would go on to achieve great things as a Gunner.

4 August

1938   Welsh international inside forward Bryn Jones joined Arsenal from Wolverhampton Wanderers in a British record £14,000 transfer deal.

1971   Referee Norman Burtenshaw reported the entire Benfica team to UEFA when he was attacked after Arsenal's 6–1 friendly win at Highbury.

1985   Stewart Robson's strike gave Arsenal a 1–1 draw against Tottenham Hotspur in Glenn Hoddle's testimonial at White Hart Lane.

1988   Two goals by David Rocastle plus another from David O'Leary saw Arsenal to a 3–1 friendly win over Anundsjo in Sweden.

1991   Sampdoria won the Makita International Tournament at Highbury, beating the Gunners 3–2 on penalties after a 1–1 draw in the final.

5 August

1946   Ian McPherson joined Arsenal from Notts County in a part-exchange deal that took fellow winger Horace Cumner to Meadow Lane.

1968   Ukraine international full back Oleg Luzhny was born in Kiev. He was a powerful athlete who could operate anywhere across the back line.

1986   Scottish champions Celtic defeated Arsenal 2–0 at Highbury in a testimonial match for Republic of Ireland international David O'Leary.

1987   Charlie Nicholas scored a hat-trick and Martin Hayes netted twice in Arsenal's 7–2 friendly victory over Brighton and Hove Albion at the Goldstone Ground.

1998   Arsène Wenger signed Argentinian full back Nelson Vivas from Swiss club Lugano. He made 40 Premiership appearances during his Highbury stint.

6 August

1926   Centre forward Harry Woods moved to Luton Town. After a spell at Kenilworth Road, the muscular Lancastrian left the Football League to join North Shields.

1966   George McLean scored twice to give Scottish Cup holders Glasgow Rangers a 2–0 friendly victory over Arsenal at Ibrox.

1977   Northern Ireland international goalkeeper Pat Jennings arrived from Tottenham Hotspur. He played for Arsenal in three successive FA Cup Finals in 1978, 1979 and 1980.

1983   Dutch international striker Robin van Persie was born in Rotterdam. He featured in Arsenal's 2005 FA Cup Final triumph.

1989   Gus Caesar was sent off and David Rocastle scored twice in Arsenal's 2–1 win over Independiente in the ZDS Challenge Trophy in Miami.

7 August

1898   Scottish centre half John Dick joined the Gunners from Airdrie in an exchange deal involving centre forward Jim Devlin.

1910   England international forward Alf Common arrived from Middlesbrough. He netted 23 goals in 77 League games for the Gunners.

1973   England winger Freddie Cox, 52, died in Bournemouth. He took a prominent role in the 1949/50 FA Cup run which culminated in Wembley victory over Liverpool.

1993   Manchester United defeated Arsenal 5–4 on penalties, after a 1–1 draw, to win the FA Charity Shield at Wembley.

1999   Dennis Bergkamp's strike plus Frank Sinclair's own-goal gave Arsenal a 2–1 Premiership win at home to Leicester City.

8 August

1959   Goals from Danny Clapton and Gerry Ward gave Arsenal a 2–2 friendly draw against Sparta Rotterdam in Holland.

1964   Billy Wright's side gained a 2–2 friendly draw against Eintracht Frankfurt with goals from George Eastham and Joe Baker.

1977   Jimmy Rimmer made his final appearance for Arsenal as Frank Stapleton's goal clinched Arsenal's 1–0 friendly win at Aldershot.

1987   Football League XI beat Rest of World 3–0 at Wembley in a match celebrating the centenary of the Football League.

2004   Gilberto Silva, Jose Antonio Reyes and Mikael Silvestre (own-goal) found the net in Arsenal's 3–1 victory over Manchester United in the FA Community Shield.

9 August

1914   England international left half Joe Mercer was born in Ellesmere Port, Cheshire. He captained Arsenal to League title glory in 1947/48 and 1952/63, and to FA Cup triumph in 1950.

1944   England Under-23 winger George Armstrong was born in Hebburn, County Durham. He netted 53 goals in a then-record 500 League games for the Gunners between 1961/62 and 1977/78.

1955   Arsenal played a cricket match against the MCC at Highbury in a benefit for footballing-cricketer Leslie Compton.

1997   Marc Overmars, Emmanuel Petit and Gilles Grimandi made their League debuts in the Gunners' 1–1 Premiership draw at Leeds United.

1998   Arsenal beat Manchester United 3–0 in the FA Charity Shield at Wembley with goals from Marc Overmars, Chris Wreh and Nicolas Anelka.

10 August

1968   John Radford's strike plus Phil Beal's own-goal gave Arsenal a 2–1 First Division victory at Tottenham Hotspur.

1974   Billy Bremner and Kevin Keegan were sent off as Leeds United faced Liverpool in the first FA Charity Shield match shown live on TV.

1994   Goalkeeper Vince Bartram was signed from AFC Bournemouth. He made 12 appearances as David Seaman's understudy before signing to Gillingham in 1997.

1999   First-half goals from Emmanuel Petit and Dennis Bergkamp earned the Gunners a 2–1 Premiership win over Derby County at Pride Park.

2003   Arsenal lost 4–3 on penalties to Manchester United after a 1–1 draw in the FA Community Shield at the Millennium Stadium.

11 August

1952   Arsenal played a cricket match against the MCC under floodlights at Highbury in a benefit for England cricketer Jack Young.

1977   Once-capped England international goalkeeper Jimmy Rimmer joined Aston Villa. He had joined Arsenal from Manchester United in 1974 and later played for Swansea City, whom he also went on to coach.

1982   England Under-21 striker Lee Chapman arrived from Stoke City. He netted six goals in 28 outings for the Gunners between 1982/83 and 1983/84 before moving to Sunderland.

1993   Ex-England Youth central defender Colin Pates moved to Brighton and Hove Albion. His peak playing days had been spent at Chelsea.

2002   Gilberto Silva scored on his debut to give Arsenal a 1–0 victory over Liverpool in the FA Community Shield.

12 August

1917   Goalkeeper Frank Boulton was born in Chipping Sodbury, Gloucestershire. He helped Arsenal to win the League title in 1937/38.

1949   Arsenal played a cricket match against the MCC at Highbury in a benefit for footballing-cricketer Denis Compton.

1989   Peter Beardsley's first-half strike gave Liverpool a hard-fought 1–0 win over Arsenal in the FA Charity Shield at Wembley.

1994   England Under-21 goalkeeper Alan Miller moved to Middlesbrough. He made eight Premiership appearances while at Highbury.

2004   England international striker Francis Jeffers moved to Charlton Athletic. He netted eight goals in 38 games for Arsenal after joining from Everton in 2001.

13 August

1958   Vic Groves and Jimmy Bloomfield scored in Arsenal's 2–1 friendly victory over Enschede Sportsclub in Holland.

1968   Two goals by Bobby Gould plus another from David Court earned the Gunners a 3–0 First Division win at home to Leicester City.

1976   Hits from Liam Brady and Trevor Ross gave Terry Neill's team a 2–2 friendly draw against Rijeka in Yugoslavia.

1980   Striker Clive Allen and goalkeeper Paul Barron moved to Crystal Palace in exchange for England international left back Kenny Sansom.

1988   Brian Marwood scored twice as George Graham's side defeated Tottenham Hotspur 4–0 in the Wembley International Tournament.

14 August

1894 England international centre half Jack Butler, capped once in 1924, was born in Colombo, Sri Lanka. He netted seven goals in 267 League games for Arsenal between 1919/20 and 1929/30.

1971 Frank McLintock, Ray Kennedy and John Radford scored in Arsenal's 3–0 First Division victory over Chelsea at Highbury.

1980 Scotland international goalkeeper George Wood, who collected four caps, arrived from Everton. He made 60 First Division appearances for Arsenal before moving on to Crystal Palace in 1983.

1988 Arsenal won the Wembley International Tournament final as Alan Smith scored twice in a 3–0 victory over Bayern Munich.

1996 Arsenal signed French international midfielders Patrick Vieira from AC Milan and Remi Garde from Strasbourg, the first of Arsène Wenger's recruits.

15 August

1965 George Eastham scored a hat-trick and George Armstrong banged in a brace in Arsenal's 6–2 friendly victory over Trinidad XI.

1970 Charlie George and George Graham were on target to give Arsenal a 2–2 First Division draw against champions Everton at Goodison Park.

1972 John Radford netted twice as Bertie Mee's side swept to a 5–2 First Division victory at home to Wolverhampton Wanderers.

1983 Striker Ian Allinson was signed from Colchester United, the club to which he returned to finish his League career in the late 1980s.

2004 Dennis Bergkamp, Jose Antonio Reyes, Freddie Ljungberg and Robert Pires all registered in Arsenal's 4–1 Premiership win at Everton.

16 August

1912   England centre forward Ted Drake was born in Southampton. He scored six times in five international outings. After retiring as a player he managed Chelsea to their first League title, in 1954/55.

1969   Charlie George scored to give Bertie Mee's side a 1–0 First Division victory over West Bromwich Albion at The Hawthorns.

1978   Midfielder John Matthews was sold to Sheffield United. He scored twice in 45 First Division games for the Gunners.

1980   Kenny Sansom made his debut as Frank Stapleton's strike clinched Arsenal's 1–0 First Division win at West Bromwich Albion.

2003   Goals from Thierry Henry and Robert Pires gave the Gunners a 2–1 Premiership victory over Everton at Highbury in the first game of their unbeaten season.

17 August

1909   England wing-half Wilf Copping was born in Barnsley, Yorkshire. During his glorious Highbury tenure he pocketed two League title medals and an FA Cup gong.

1977   French international striker Thierry Henry was born in Paris. He was destined to break Arsenal's all-time goalscoring record (see 18 October, page 153).

1990   Goals by David Rocastle and Alan Smith gave Arsenal a 2–2 away draw against Brighton and Hove Albion in Steve Gatting's testimonial match.

1996   John Hartson and Dennis Bergkamp netted in the Gunners' 2–0 Premiership victory over West Ham United at Highbury.

1998   Arsène Wenger's side gained a 2–1 Premiership win at home to Nottingham Forest with goals from Emmanuel Petit and Marc Overmars.

18 August

1962   Joe Baker netted brilliantly on his League debut for Arsenal in a 2–1 First Division victory over newly promoted Leyton Orient at Brisbane Road.

1973   Derek Dougan scored twice as Wolverhampton Wanderers gained a 3–1 FA Cup third-place play-off win over Arsenal at Highbury.

1979   Two goals by Alan Sunderland plus others from Frank Stapleton and Liam Brady gave Arsenal a 4–0 First Division win at the Goldstone Ground against Brighton and Hove Albion.

1988   Ian Rush rejoined Liverpool from Juventus for £2,800,000. The Welsh international scored 228 goals in 469 League games overall.

2001   A brace by Dennis Bergkamp plus strikes from Thierry Henry and Robert Pires secured a 4–0 Premiership victory at Middlesbrough.

19 August

1956   Full back Joe Wade was appointed player-manager of Hereford United. He picked up a title medal in 1952/53 and represented the Football League.

1961   Laurie Brown made his debut as Mel Charles scored twice in Arsenal's 2–2 First Division draw against Burnley at Highbury.

1966   England inside forward George Eastham, who collected 19 caps, joined Stoke City. He netted 41 goals in 223 outings for Arsenal between 1960/61 and 1965/66 and was awarded the OBE in 1973 for his services to football.

1972   Ray Kennedy netted both goals as Bertie Mee's team gained a 2–0 First Division victory over Stoke City at Highbury.

1975   Strikes by Liam Brady, Pat Rice and Brian Kidd gave the Gunners a 3–1 First Division win over Sheffield United at Bramall Lane.

20 August

1966   Two goals by Alan Skirton plus another from George Armstrong earned Arsenal a 3–1 First Division victory away to Sunderland.

1973   Goals from Charlie George and John Radford gave Arsenal a 2–1 friendly triumph over Glasgow Rangers at Ibrox.

1985   Tommy Caton, Stewart Robson and Tony Woodcock scored in the Gunners' 3–2 First Division win at home to Southampton.

1994   Strikes by Kevin Campbell and Ian Wright plus Tony Coton's own-goal secured a 3–0 Premiership win over Manchester City at Highbury.

1995   Ian Wright scored as Bruce Rioch's first Premiership match as Arsenal's manager ended in a 1–1 draw at home to Middlesbrough.

21 August

1956   Goals from Mike Tiddy and Jimmy Bloomfield gave Arsenal a 2–0 First Division victory over Burnley at Highbury.

1965   Keith Peacock became the first substitute in the Football League when he came on for Charlton Athletic against Bolton Wanderers.

1981   Republic of Ireland international striker Frank Stapleton moved from Arsenal to Manchester United after scoring 108 goals in 299 games for the Gunners from 1974/75 to 1980/81.

1992   Winger Perry Groves moved from Arsenal to Southampton. The wiry redhead was renowned for his energy and phenomenal work rate.

2000   Patrick Vieira was sent off but goals from Lauren and Thierry Henry gave Arsenal a 2–0 Premiership win at home to Liverpool.

22 August

1951   Cliff Holton, Ben Marden and Don Roper scored in the Gunners' 3–1 First Division victory over Chelsea at Stamford Bridge.

1953   Gerry Ward, at 16 years 321 days, became Arsenal's youngest ever League debutant in the 0–0 draw at home to Huddersfield Town.

1964   Liverpool gained a 3–2 First Division victory over Arsenal at Anfield in the first game screened on BBC's *Match of the Day*.

1970   John Radford's hat-trick plus a goal by George Graham earned Arsenal a thumping 4–0 First Division win over Manchester United at Highbury.

2004   Arsenal trailed 3–1 to Middlesbrough after 53 minutes before fighting back to secure a thrilling 5–3 Premiership victory at Highbury.

23 August

1920   England left back Lionel Smith was born in Mexborough, Yorkshire. After giving his all as a Gunner, he served Watford and later ran a pub in Stoke Newington.

1947   Archie Macaulay and Don Roper made their debuts as Arsenal gained a 3–1 First Division win over Sunderland at Highbury.

1958   Scotland international wing-half Tommy Docherty, who played 25 times for his country, joined from Preston North End on the day Arsenal lost 2–1 at Deepdale.

1986   George Graham's managerial reign kicked off well as Charlie Nicholas' goal clinched a 1–0 First Division win at home to Manchester United.

1992   Arsenal earned their first Premier League points as Anders Limpar and Ian Wright scored in a 2–0 win over Liverpool at Anfield.

24 August

1954   Marksman David Herd was signed from Stockport County. He had played alongside his father Alex for the Edgeley Park club.

1961   George Armstrong signed on as an Arsenal professional under George Swindin. The winger netted 53 goals in 500 First Division games while at Highbury.

1967   England international midfielder Michael Thomas was born in Lambeth, London. He netted 30 goals in 206 outings for Arsenal, including the famous title-clincher at Anfield in 1989.

2000   French international striker Sylvain Wiltord was signed from Bordeaux. He scored 49 times in 173 games for Arsenal between 2000/01 and 2003/04.

2003   Two goals by Sylvain Wiltord plus others from Thierry Henry and Gilberto Silva gave Arsenal a 4–0 Premiership win at Middlesbrough.

25 August

1934   Wilf Copping made his debut as Ray Bowden, Ted Drake and Cliff Bastin notched in Arsenal's tense 3–3 First Division draw away to Portsmouth.

1973   Ray Kennedy, John Radford and Alan Ball were on target in the Gunners' 3–0 First Division win at home to Manchester United.

1990   Goals from Paul Merson, Alan Smith and Perry Groves saw Arsenal to a 3–0 First Division victory over Wimbledon at Plough Lane.

2001   Freddie Ljungberg, Sylvain Wiltord, Thierry Henry and Kanu netted in Arsenal's 4–0 Premiership win over Leicester City at Highbury.

2004   Strikes by Thierry Henry, Cesc Fabregas and Jose Antonio Reyes gave Arsenal a 3–0 Premiership victory at home to Blackburn Rovers.

26 August

1904 England winger Joe Hulme was born in Stafford. He was a key figure in Arsenal's successes under Herbert Chapman.

1913 England winger Alf Kirchen was born in Shouldham, Norfolk. His career was ended by a serious knee injury suffered playing football during the war.

1958 Scotland international wing-half Tommy Docherty scored on his debut in Arsenal's 3–0 First Division win at home to Burnley.

1987 Midfielder Kevin Richardson arrived from Watford. He helped the Gunners lift the League crown in 1988/89 and was capped once by England as an Aston Villa man in 1994.

2000 Patrick Vieira and Thierry Henry netted two goals apiece as Arsenal gained a 5–3 Premiership victory at home to Charlton Athletic.

27 August

1919 Winger Joe Toner joined Arsenal from Belfast United and remained at Highbury from 1919 to 1926. Later he excelled for St Johnstone, then crossed the Irish Sea to Coleraine.

1988 Steve Bould made his debut as Alan Smith grabbed a hat-trick in Arsenal's thumping 5–1 First Division victory away to FA Cup winners Wimbledon.

1997 Dennis Bergkamp notched a splendid hat-trick, one goal of which won Goal of the Season, in the Gunners' dramatic 3–3 Premiership draw against Leicester City.

1999 Portuguese striker Luis Boa Morte moved to Southampton. He made 35 appearances while at Highbury and netted four goals.

2002 Sylvain Wiltord scored twice as Arsenal gained a 5–2 Premiership victory at home to newly promoted West Bromwich Albion.

28 August

1926   Tom Parker and Charlie Buchan found the net to earn Herbert Chapman's side a 2–1 First Division victory at home to Derby County.

1937   Ted Drake's hat-trick plus a goal by Cliff Bastin secured Arsenal a convincing 4–1 First Division win over Everton at Goodison Park.

1967   Jon Sammels' strike and Tony Hateley's own-goal gave the Gunners a 2–0 First Division victory over Liverpool at Highbury.

1993   Arsenal gained their fourth successive Premiership win as Ian Wright scored twice in a 2–0 victory at home to Everton.

2004   Jose Antonio Reyes, Thierry Henry, Robert Pires and Dennis Bergkamp all registered in Arsenal's 4–1 Premiership win at Norwich City.

29 August

1925   Arsenal suffered a 1–0 defeat at home to local rivals Tottenham Hotspur in their first League match under Herbert Chapman.

1959   Two goals by David Herd plus another from Danny Clapton saw the Gunners to a 3–3 First Division draw away to Wolverhampton Wanderers.

1961   Johnny MacLeod, George Eastham, Alan Skirton and Mel Charles all hit the target in Arsenal's nerve-shredding 4–4 First Division draw at home to Leicester City.

1978   Goals by Dave Gwyther, John Green and Richard Finney earned Rotherham United a shock 3–1 League Cup second-round win over Arsenal at Millmoor.

1987   Kevin Richardson made his debut as Alan Smith plundered a hat-trick in Arsenal's handsome 6–0 First Division win over Portsmouth at Highbury.

30 August

1920 Strikes by Fred Pagnam and Jimmy Smith gave the Gunners a 2–0 First Division win over Manchester United at Highbury.

1930 Cliff Bastin and David Jack scored two goals each in Arsenal's 4–1 First Division victory over Blackpool at Bloomfield Road.

1955 Tranmere Rovers centre half Harold Bell finally missed a League match after playing a record 401 consecutive post-war games.

1977 Two goals by Malcolm Macdonald plus another from Liam Brady gave Arsenal a 3–2 League Cup second-round win over Manchester United.

1980 Terry Neill's side gained a 2–0 First Division win at home to Tottenham Hotspur with goals from David Price and Frank Stapleton.

31 August

1927 Two goals by Jimmy Brain plus others from Charlie Buchan and Billy Blyth secured Arsenal a 4–1 First Division win over Burnley.

1929 Scotland international Alex James made his debut and David Jack scored twice in Arsenal's swinging 4–0 First Division win at Leeds United.

1935 Jackie Milne made his Arsenal entrance as Ted Drake netted twice in the Gunners' 3–1 First Division victory at home to Sunderland.

1946 Football League games resumed after the Second World War, with identical fixtures to the first day of the aborted 1939/40 campaign.

2003 Second-half strikes from Sylvain Wiltord and Freddie Ljungberg gave leaders Arsenal a 2–1 Premiership win at Manchester City.

1 September

1897 Twice-capped Irish international left back Andy Kennedy was born in Belfast. He carved a reputation with Glentoran and Crystal Palace before joining the Gunners.

1934 Jack Crayston made his debut as Ted Drake and Ray Bowden helped themselves to hat-tricks in Arsenal's 8–1 greatest ever thrashing of Liverpool.

1953 Goalkeeper Ted Platt moved from Arsenal to Portsmouth after 53 First Division appearances for the Gunners.

1983 Spanish international striker Jose Antonio Reyes was born in Utrera. He featured in Arsenal's 2005 FA Cup Final success against Manchester United.

2001 Arsenal pair David Seaman and Ashley Cole excelled in England's historic 5–1 World Cup qualifying win over Germany in Munich.

2 September

1893 Goals by Walter Shaw and Arthur Elliott gave the Gunners a 2–2 draw at home to Newcastle United in their first League match.

1961 England Under-21 central defender Chris Whyte was born in Islington, London. He netted eight goals in 113 outings for Arsenal from 1981/82 to 1985/86.

1964 Scotland winger Johnny MacLeod joined Aston Villa. After his spell in the Midlands, he played in Belgium before finishing his career in his homeland, with Raith Rovers.

1976 Scotland Under-23 midfielder Eddie Kelly was sold to QPR. He was instrumental in Arsenal's 1970/71 Double success, scoring in the FA Cup Final.

1978 Graham Rix and Frank Stapleton netted two goals apiece as the Gunners gained a 5–1 First Division win at home to QPR.

3 September

1927   Charlie Buchan scored twice as Herbert Chapman's side stormed to a 6–1 First Division win over Sheffield United at Highbury.

1932   England international Joe Hulme smashed a hat-trick in the Gunners' 6–1 First Division drubbing of Sunderland at Highbury.

1947   Reg Lewis scored four goals and Ronnie Rooke netted twice in Arsenal's 6–0 First Division annihilation of Charlton Athletic at Highbury.

1977   Richie Powling made his final appearance as Frank Stapleton scored twice in Arsenal's 3–0 First Division home win over Nottingham Forest.

1991   Alan Smith netted a brace to give George Graham's team a 2–2 First Division draw against Leeds United at Elland Road.

4 September

1891   Centre forward Fred Pagnam was born in Poulton-le-Fylde, Lancashire. After leaving the Gunners, he served Watford as player and manager, then coached in Turkey and Holland.

1937   Ted Drake scored twice as George Allison's side gained a 5–0 First Division win at home to Wolverhampton Wanderers.

1968   Goalkeeper Jim Furnell was sold to Rotherham United. He made 141 First Division appearances during a solid Highbury stint.

1979   Alan Sunderland knocked in a hat-trick and Liam Brady contributed two penalties in Arsenal's remarkable 7–0 League Cup second-round replay win over Leeds United.

1986   Striker Perry Groves arrived from Colchester United. His uncle, Vic Groves, had a spell as Arsenal's captain in the late 1950s.

5 September

1891 Royal Arsenal's first match after turning professional ended in a 2–0 friendly defeat at home to Sheffield United.

1927 Strikes by Billy Blyth and Jimmy Brain gave Herbert Chapman's side a 2–1 First Division victory over Burnley at Turf Moor.

1934 Two goals by Ted Drake plus others from Ray Bowden and Cliff Bastin earned Arsenal a 4–0 First Division win at home to Blackburn Rovers.

1942 Alf Kirchen netted a hat-trick in Arsenal's 6–1 wartime Football League South victory over Southampton at Highbury.

1970 George Armstrong bagged a brace in the first half, enabling Bertie Mee's side to gain a 2–0 First Division victory over Tottenham Hotspur at Highbury.

6 September

1913 Goals from George Jobey and Archie Devine secured a 2–1 First Division win for Woolwich Arsenal, as the Club were still known, against Leicester Fosse in the first match at Highbury.

1958 David Herd scored four times as George Swindin's team cruised to a 6–1 First Division victory over Everton at Highbury.

1967 George Armstrong, Jon Sammels and Colin Addison netted in Arsenal's 3–1 First Division win at West Bromwich Albion.

1983 Tottenham Hotspur's 3.8 million shares were quickly snapped up after going on sale, the first football club quoted on the Stock Exchange.

2000 Arsenal fought back from two goals down as Thierry Henry and Silvinho scored in an exciting 2–2 Premiership draw at Chelsea.

7 September

1908   David Neave, Harry Lee and Sam Raybould scored to give the Gunners a 3–0 First Division win against Everton at Goodison Park.

1945   England midfielder Peter Storey, who accumulated 19 caps in the early 1970s, was born in Farnham, Surrey. As a Gunner he scored 17 times in 501 outings between 1965/66 and 1976/77.

1963   Two goals by Alan Skirton plus others from Joe Baker and Ian Ure saw Arsenal through to a nail-biting 4–3 First Division win over Bolton Wanderers.

1985   Tony Woodcock and Charlie Nicholas netted in Arsenal's 2–0 First Division victory over Coventry City at Highfield Road.

1996   Second-half strikes by Paul Merson and Andy Linighan earned the Gunners a 2–2 Premiership draw at Aston Villa.

8 September

1906   Charlie Satterthwaite netted both goals as Phil Kelso's team secured a 2–0 First Division victory at home to Middlesbrough.

1914   Two goals by Harry King plus others from John Flanagan and Frank Bradshaw gave Arsenal a 4–0 First Division win at Glossop North End, who exited the League in 1915.

1956   Jimmy Bloomfield, Mike Tiddy and Cliff Holton scored to give the Gunners a 3–2 First Division victory away to Portsmouth.

1984   Brian Talbot scored twice as Arsenal's 3–1 win over Liverpool put them top of the First Division for the first time in 12 years.

1990   Arsenal maintained their unbeaten start to the season as Perry Groves scored to clinch a 1–1 First Division draw at Everton.

9 September

1958   Gordon Nutt poached a brace as George Swindin's side charged to a 6–1 First Division victory at home to Bolton Wanderers.

1969   Arsenal began their triumphant European Fairs Cup campaign as George Graham netted twice in a 3–0 first-round first-leg win over Northern Ireland's Glentoran.

1981   Midfielder Steve Gatting was sold to Brighton and Hove Albion. He played for the Seagulls in their FA Cup Final defeat (after a replay) to Manchester United in 1983.

1989   Paul Merson, Alan Smith, Michael Thomas, Tony Adams and Brian Marwood all scored in Arsenal's 5–0 First Division demolition of Sheffield Wednesday at Highbury.

2000   Sylvain Wiltord started his first match for Arsenal and Ashley Cole's equalizer clinched a 1–1 Premiership draw away to Bradford City.

10 September

1931   Centre forward Jimmy Brain moved to Tottenham Hotspur. He scored 125 times in 204 League games for the Gunners.

1968   Arsenal right back Pat Rice gained the first of his 49 caps for Northern Ireland in the 3–2 victory over Israel in Jaffa.

1980   Arsenal midfielder Graham Rix made his England debut in the 4–0 World Cup qualifier win over Norway at Wembley. He went on to collect 17 caps.

1988   Nigel Winterburn, Brian Marwood and Alan Smith scored in Arsenal's 3–2 First Division victory at Tottenham Hotspur.

2002   Arsenal equalled a 65-year-old League record with a 2–1 win at home to Manchester City, having scored in 44 consecutive League matches.

11 September

1893 John Heath grabbed a hat-trick as Woolwich Arsenal gained their first win in the Football League, beating Walsall Town Swifts 4–0.

1935 Jackie Milne hit the target three times as George Allison's side swept to a superb 6–0 First Division victory at home to Grimsby Town.

1946 Welsh international central defender John Roberts was born in Swansea. He was a member of Arsenal's 1970/71 Double-winning squad, playing in half of that season's matches.

1993 Kevin Campbell's hat-trick plus a goal by Ian Wright gave Arsenal a 4–0 Premiership victory at home to Ipswich Town.

1999 Croatian international Davor Suker scored his first two goals for Arsenal in a 3–1 Premiership win over Aston Villa at Highbury.

12 September

1912 Twice-capped England centre half Leslie Compton was born in Woodford, Essex. The brother of Test cricket star and Arsenal forward Denis Compton, he netted five goals in 253 League outings for the Gunners.

1929 Winger Sid Hoar moved from Arsenal to Clapton Orient of the Third Division South. He scored 16 times in 100 First Division games for the Gunners.

1953 Goalkeeper George Swindin, later to manage the Gunners, made his final appearance as Arsenal suffered a 7–1 First Division reverse away to Sunderland.

1966 Winger Alan Skirton was sold to Blackpool. He had recovered from tuberculosis as a 20-year-old to enjoy a successful career as a pacy, powerful goalscoring winger.

2000 Silvinho's outstanding individual goal clinched Arsenal's 1–0 UEFA Champions League Group B victory at Sparta Prague.

13 September

1909   England inside or centre forward Ray Bowden, who earned six caps, was born in Looe, Cornwall. He netted 42 goals in 123 League outings while at Highbury.

1949   Winger Freddie Cox arrived from local rivals Tottenham Hotspur. He scored FA Cup semi-final goals in 1950 and 1952 as Arsenal reached both finals.

1977   England Under-23 winger George Armstrong was sold to Leicester City. At Filbert Street he was reunited with Frank McLintock, a fellow member of the great 1970/71 Double side.

1978   Frank Stapleton scored twice in the Gunners' 3–0 UEFA Cup first-round first-leg victory over German side Lokomotiv Leipzig at Highbury.

1997   Ian Wright stroked a hat-trick in Arsenal's 4–1 Premiership win at home to Bolton Wanderers, finally beating Cliff Bastin's goals record.

14 September

1901   Scottish inside left Alex James was born in Mossend, Lanarkshire. The baggy-shorted schemer was the midfield brains behind the team's astonishing success in the 1930s.

1923   Inside left Doug Lishman was born in Birmingham. He was at his most effective during his Highbury years in a left-flank partnership with winger Don Roper.

1929   Jack Lambert scored twice as Herbert Chapman's side gained a crushing 6–1 First Division victory over Burnley at Highbury.

1991   Two goals by Kevin Campbell plus others from Alan Smith and Michael Thomas gave Arsenal a 4–1 First Division win away to Crystal Palace.

2005   Arsenal began their UEFA Champions League campaign winning 2–1 at home to FC Thun with goals by Gilberto and Dennis Bergkamp.

15 September

1890   Arsenal left back Arthur Hutchins was born in Bishop's Waltham, Hampshire. He joined the Gunners from non-League Croydon Common for £50 in 1919.

1934   Ray Bowden, Alex James, Cliff Bastin and Ted Drake all netted to give Arsenal a thrilling 4–3 First Division home win over West Bromwich Albion.

1973   Arsenal earned a comfortable 4–0 First Division win at Norwich City with goals from Charlie George, Bob McNab, Alan Ball and Ray Kennedy.

1990   Anders Limpar, Lee Dixon, Paul Merson and David Rocastle all registered in the Gunners' 4–1 First Division victory at home to Chelsea.

2001   Strikes by Freddie Ljungberg, Thierry Henry and Dennis Bergkamp secured Arsène Wenger's side a 3–1 Premiership victory away to Fulham.

16 September

1937   Arsenal's first team played the reserves in a practice game shown on the BBC, the first football match to be shown live on TV.

1967   Goals by John Radford, Terry Neill, George Graham and Colin Addison gave Arsenal an easy 4–0 First Division win over Tottenham Hotspur.

1972   Jimmy Hill abandoned his job as a commentator to replace an injured linesman during Arsenal's 0–0 draw with Liverpool.

1996   Arsène Wenger was officially named as Arsenal's new manager, then Ian Wright scored a hat-trick in a 4–1 Premiership home win over Sheffield Wednesday.

1998   Tony Adams returned for his first match of the season as Arsenal lost 1–0 at PAOK Salonika in the UEFA Cup first-round first leg.

17 September

1898   The Gunners secured a 4–1 Second Division win at Darwen with goals from Fergus Hunt, Hugh Dailly, Billy White and John Anderson.

1932   Joe Hulme, Tim Coleman and Cliff Bastin scored in the Gunners' 3–2 First Division victory at home to Bolton Wanderers.

1960   Geoff Strong netted on his League debut as Arsenal surged to a 5–0 First Division win over Newcastle United at Highbury.

1983   Strikes by Graham Rix, Tony Woodcock and Brian Talbot, supplemented by a David Hunt own-goal, gave Arsenal a 4–0 First Division win away to Notts County.

1998   Swedish international midfielder Freddie Ljungberg was signed from Halmstad. He became an instant Highbury favourite by scoring on his debut against Manchester United.

18 September

1953   The great England centre forward Tommy Lawton was signed from Brentford. He netted 13 goals in 35 League games for Arsenal.

1974   England central defender Sol Campbell was born in Newham, London. He was signed from Tottenham Hotspur in the summer of 2001.

1976   England Under-21 midfielder Stephen Hughes was born in Reading. He helped to win the FA Youth Cup in 1994 and made a promising start to his Highbury career, then joined Everton in 2000.

1990   European debutant Alan Smith scored four goals as Arsenal trounced FK Austria 6–1 at Highbury in the European Cup first-round first leg.

1999   Thierry Henry kicked off his goalscoring feats for Arsenal in a 1–0 Premiership win over Southampton at The Dell.

19 September

1937 Arsenal inside forward Geoff Strong was born in Kirkheaton, Northumberland. He was the Gunners' leading marksman in League games in 1963/64.

1951 Cliff Holton grabbed a hat-trick as Arsenal trounced Hapoel Tel Aviv 6–1 in their first floodlit friendly match staged at Highbury.

1963 England goalkeeper David Seaman was born in Rotherham, Yorkshire. He accumulated nine major club honours during his regal sojourn with the Gunners.

1970 Ray Kennedy and George Graham scored two goals apiece as Arsenal gained a 6–2 First Division home victory over West Bromwich Albion.

2001 Two goals by Thierry Henry plus another from Freddie Ljungberg gave Arsenal a 3–2 UEFA Champions League Group C win over German side Schalke.

20 September

1952 Scotland international goalkeeper George Wood was born in Douglas, Lanarkshire. Before joining the Gunners in 1980 he served East Stirlingshire, Blackpool and Everton.

1962 Once-capped England winger Danny Clapton was sold to Luton Town. Before joining the Gunners he had worked as a porter at Billingsgate market.

1996 Republic of Ireland international Eddie McGoldrick joined Manchester City. Before arriving at Highbury in summer 1993 he had served Northampton Town and Crystal Palace and won 15 caps for his country.

1998 Tony Adams, Nicolas Anelka and Freddie Ljungberg hit the target in Arsenal's 3–0 Premiership win over Manchester United at Highbury.

2000 Martin Keown scored twice in the last five minutes as Arsenal gained a dramatic 3–2 UEFA Champions League Group B win over Ukrainian club Shakhtjor Donetsk.

21 September

1949   England lost their first international at home to non-British opposition, when beaten 1–0 by the Republic of Ireland at Goodison Park.

1970   French international midfielder Emmanuel Petit was born in Dieppe. He scored 11 times in 116 games for Arsenal and played a major part in the Gunners' Double triumph in his first Highbury campaign.

1990   England winger Brian Marwood, who earned one cap in 1988, moved to Sheffield United. He featured prominently in Arsenal's 1988/89 League title success.

1991   Lee Dixon, Kevin Campbell, David Rocastle, Alan Smith and Perry Groves all scored in the 5–2 First Division win over Sheffield United at Highbury.

1997   Two goals by Dennis Bergkamp and Nigel Winterburn's late strike gave Arsène Wenger's side a 3–2 Premiership victory away to Chelsea.

22 September

1891   England inside forward Charlie Buchan was born in Plumstead, London. Capped six times, he skippered Arsenal in the 1927 FA Cup Final, which was lost to Cardiff City.

1954   Arsenal left half Dave Bowen gained the first of his 19 caps for Wales in the 3–1 defeat by Yugoslavia in Cardiff.

1956   Jimmy Bloomfield scored twice as Tom Whittaker's team earned a 4–2 First Division victory over Sheffield Wednesday at Hillsborough.

1984   Two goals by Tony Woodcock plus others from Paul Mariner and Kenny Sansom gave Arsenal a 4–0 First Division win over Stoke City at Highbury.

1999   Late strikes by Thierry Henry and Davor Suker kept Arsenal's UEFA Champions League bid on course with a 3–1 win over AIK Stockholm at Wembley.

23 September

1922   Reg Boreham netted twice to give Leslie Knighton's team a 2–1 First Division win over Tottenham Hotspur at White Hart Lane.

1936   England inside forward George Eastham was born in Blackpool. His father, also George, played for his country some three decades earlier in 1935. They were the first father and son to represent England.

1955   Wingers Gordon Nutt and Mike Tiddy joined Arsenal in a package deal from First Division rivals Cardiff City.

1970   John Radford and George Armstrong scored as holders Arsenal beat Lazio 2–0 in the second leg of the European Fairs Cup first round, winning 4–2 on aggregate.

1995   Dennis Bergkamp scored two exceptional goals, his first for Arsenal, in the 4–2 Premiership victory over Southampton at Highbury.

24 September

1904   Charlie Satterthwaite scored Arsenal's first-ever goal in the First Division in a 2–0 win at home to Wolverhampton Wanderers.

1965   Swedish international winger Anders Limpar, bought by George Graham to add a new dimension to Arsenal's attack, was born in Solna.

1981   Northern Ireland international left back Sammy Nelson joined Brighton and Hove Albion after playing for Arsenal in three successive FA Cup Finals.

1991   England striker Ian Wright was signed from Crystal Palace. During a scintillating Highbury sojourn, he made nonsense of doubters who believed Arsenal were foolhardy to pay the high transfer fee for a 27-year-old.

1997   Marc Overmars scored twice as leaders Arsenal swept to a 4–0 Premiership victory over West Ham United at Highbury.

25 September

1962   Arsenal triumphed 3–0 in the last of the annual fixtures against Racing Club Paris. The Gunners won 19 of the 27 games.

1963   Geoff Strong and Joe Baker plundered hat-tricks in Arsenal's expansive 7–1 European Fairs Cup first-round first-leg win over Staevnet in Denmark.

1965   Joe Baker, John Radford, George Armstrong and George Eastham all netted in Arsenal's 4–2 First Division victory over Manchester United at Highbury.

1968   Dave Jenkins grabbed a hat-trick as Arsenal stormed to a 6–1 League Cup third-round triumph away to Scunthorpe United.

2002   Gilberto Silva scored the fastest-ever UEFA Champions League goal, after just 19 seconds, in Arsenal's 4–0 Group A victory at PSV Eindhoven.

26 September

1925   Two goals by Jimmy Brain plus others from Charlie Buchan and Andy Neil earned Arsenal a 4–1 First Division win over Leeds United.

1938   Ted Drake scored a brace to give the Gunners a 2–1 victory over Preston North End in the FA Charity Shield at Highbury.

1953   Doug Lishman netted twice for the third successive match as Arsenal gained a 3–0 First Division victory away to Cardiff City.

1958   England left back Kenny Sansom was born in Camberwell, London. He scored six goals in 394 games for the Gunners from 1980/81 to 1987/88 and won a then-Club-record 77 caps while at Highbury.

2003   Two goals by Thierry Henry plus another from Gilberto Silva gave leaders Arsenal a 3–2 Premiership home win over Newcastle United.

27 September

1902   Billy Gooing netted a hat-trick as Harry Bradshaw's team gained a 6–1 Second Division victory at home to Gainsborough Trinity.

1908   England international left back Eddie Hapgood was born in Bristol. He helped Arsenal win the League Championship five times.

1930   Jack Lambert's hat-trick plus a goal by Cliff Bastin gave Arsenal a 4–2 First Division victory over Birmingham City at St Andrews.

1978   Frank Stapleton scored twice as Arsenal won 4–1 at Lokomotiv Leipzig in the UEFA Cup first-round second leg to triumph 7–1 on aggregate (see September 13, page 136, for first leg).

2005   Goals from Freddie Ljungberg and Robert Pires gave the Gunners a 2–1 UEFA Champions League victory over Ajax in Holland.

28 September

1966   Tommy Baldwin and George Armstrong netted two goals apiece in the 5–0 League Cup second-round second-replay win over Gillingham at Highbury.

1970   Ray Kennedy scored twice as Bertie Mee's side cruised to a 4–0 League Cup second-round replay victory at home to Ipswich Town.

1981   Former Liverpool manager Bill Shankly died aged 67. The darling of the Kop had turned Liverpool into one of the greatest clubs.

1991   Ian Wright scored a hat-trick on his League debut for Arsenal in a 4–0 First Division win over Southampton at The Dell.

2002   Arsenal won 4–1 at Leeds United to set an astounding and impressive League record by scoring in 47 consecutive games, remaining unbeaten in 23 away matches and 29 Premiership fixtures.

29 September

1894 Henry Boyd's hat-trick and a goal by Peter Mortimer saw the Gunners to a 4–2 Second Division win at home to Manchester City.

1934 Four goals by Ted Drake plus another from Cliff Bastin gave Arsenal a 5–1 First Division victory over Birmingham City at Highbury.

1971 John Radford scored twice as Arsenal prevailed 4–0 at Highbury to Norwegian team Stromsgodset in the second leg of the European Cup first round to triumph 7–1 on aggregate.

1984 Arsenal gained a 2–1 First Division victory over Coventry City at Highfield Road with goals from Tony Woodcock and Paul Mariner.

2001 Richard Wright made his Premiership debut for Arsenal and Thierry Henry netted twice to secure a 2–0 victory at Derby County.

30 September

1933 Ralph Birkett and David Jack scored two goals apiece in the Gunners' 6–0 First Division victory over Middlesbrough at Highbury.

1950 Two goals by Doug Lishman plus another from Jimmy Logie gave Arsenal a 3–0 First Division win at home over West Bromwich Albion.

1966 George Graham was signed from Chelsea. 'Stroller' netted 77 goals in 308 outings for Arsenal from 1966/67 to 1972/73, and starred in the Double triumph of 1970/71.

1978 David O'Leary, David Price and Steve Walford scored in Arsenal's 3–2 First Division victory over Middlesbrough at Ayresome Park.

1998 Congestion delayed the kick-off, then 73,455 fans saw Arsenal beat Panathinaikos 2–1 at Wembley in the UEFA Champions League Group E.

1 October

1957   Arsenal striker Ian Allinson was born in Stevenage, Hertfordshire. His most productive campaign as a Gunner was 1984/85, when he enjoyed a purple patch of eight goals in 11 outings.

1966   Left back Bob McNab was signed from Huddersfield Town. He won four England caps while at Highbury and scored 6 goals in 365 appearances for the Gunners before leaving to join Wolves in 1975.

1969   Ex-England Youth goalkeeper Geoff Barnett arrived from Everton. He played for Arsenal in the 1972 FA Cup Final, which was lost to Leeds United.

1981   Bryan Robson followed Ron Atkinson from West Bromwich Albion to Manchester United for a British record of £1,500,000.

2000   Thierry Henry's strike gave Arsenal a 1–0 victory at home to Manchester United, the visitors' first Premiership defeat for eight months.

2 October

1937   Jackie Milne and Alf Kirchen netted to give Arsenal a 2–1 First Division win at home to reigning champions Manchester City.

1954   Two goals by Tommy Lawton plus another from Jimmy Logie earned Arsenal an exciting 3–3 First Division draw at Leicester City.

1957   Ray Swallow, Mike Tiddy, Jimmy Bloomfield and David Herd all scored in Arsenal's 4–0 First Division victory over Aston Villa.

1976   Arsenal gained a 3–2 First Division win at home to QPR with goals from Pat Rice, Liam Brady and Frank Stapleton.

2004   Thierry Henry scored twice as leaders Arsenal stormed to a 4–0 Premiership victory over Charlton Athletic at Highbury.

3 October

1903 Tommy Shanks, Tim Coleman, Walter Busby and Tom Briercliffe all registered in the 4–0 Second Division triumph over Manchester United.

1953 Don Roper scored twice as Tom Whittaker's side gained a 3–2 First Division victory at home to title rivals Preston North End.

1958 Scotland international attacker Jackie Henderson arrived from Wolverhampton Wanderers. He did well for Arsenal, but he had enjoyed his prime form with his first club, Portsmouth.

1970 Ray Kennedy netted his first hat-trick for the Gunners as they swept to a 4–0 First Division win at home to Nottingham Forest.

1989 Michael Thomas grabbed a hat-trick as Arsenal won 6–1 at Plymouth Argyle in the Littlewoods Cup second-round second leg.

4 October

1919 Leeds City were expelled from the Football League after irregular payments to players. Port Vale took over their fixtures and results.

1942 Republic of Ireland international central defender Terry Mancini was born in St Pancras, London. He scored one goal in 62 appearances for the Gunners between 1974/75 and 1975/76.

1958 Jackie Henderson scored twice on his debut as Arsenal gained a thrilling 4–3 First Division win at home to West Bromwich Albion.

1986 Steve Williams scored direct from a corner as Arsenal clinched a 1–0 First Division win over Everton at Goodison Park.

1998 Dennis Bergkamp hit the target twice and missed a penalty in the Gunners' 3–0 Premiership victory at home to Newcastle United.

5 October

1889   Humphrey Barbour and Billy Scott netted hat-tricks as the Gunners trounced Lyndhurst 11–0 in the Club's first-ever FA Cup tie.

1935   Ray Bowden grabbed a hat-trick as George Allison's team gained a 5–1 First Division win over Blackburn Rovers at Highbury.

1946   Len Shackleton scored six goals on his debut after moving from Bradford PA as Newcastle United beat Newport County 13–0.

1963   Geoff Strong scored a hat-trick and Joe Baker poached a brace in Arsenal's crunching 6–0 First Division victory at home to Ipswich Town.

1964   Scotland international Frank McLintock, capped nine times, joined from Leicester City. He was Arsenal captain during the Double glory of 1970/71.

6 October

1948   Two goals by Reg Lewis plus others from Ronnie Rooke and Bryn Jones gave Arsenal a 4–3 win over Manchester United in the FA Charity Shield at Wembley.

1956   Cliff Holton scored four times as the Gunners stormed to a 7–3 First Division victory over Manchester City at Highbury.

1962   David Court scored twice as Arsenal came back from three down to gain a 4–4 First Division draw at Tottenham Hotspur.

1966   Republic of Ireland striker Niall Quinn, who collected 91 caps, was born in Dublin. He featured in Arsenal's 1987 Littlewoods Cup Final success against Liverpool and scored 20 goals for the Club between 1985/86 and 1989/90.

2002   Two goals by Kanu plus another from Patrick Vieira gave leaders Arsenal a 3–1 Premiership victory at home to Sunderland.

7 October

1922 Goals from Bert White, Clem Voysey and Reg Boreham earned the Gunners a 3–1 First Division win over West Bromwich Albion.

1931 Cliff Bastin's strike clinched Arsenal's 1–0 victory over West Bromwich Albion in the FA Charity Shield at Villa Park.

1950 Peter Goring, Alex Forbes and Don Roper scored to give Arsenal a 3–1 First Division win over Charlton Athletic at The Valley.

1961 Two goals by Mel Charles plus another from Gerry Ward saw the Gunners to a 3–0 First Division victory at home to Blackpool.

1992 The Gunners defeated Millwall 3–1 on penalties after a 1–1 draw in the Coca-Cola League Cup second-round second leg at The Den.

8 October

1930 Strikes by Joe Hulme and David Jack gave Arsenal a 2–1 victory over Sheffield Wednesday in the FA Charity Shield at Stamford Bridge.

1936 Winger Pat Beasley moved from Arsenal to Huddersfield Town. He helped the Gunners to win successive League titles in 1933/34 and 1934/35.

1949 Peter Goring and Reg Lewis scored two goals apiece as Arsenal secured a 5–2 First Division victory over Everton at Highbury.

1991 George Graham signed winger Jimmy Carter from Liverpool, but he wasn't on his best form at Highbury and moved on to Portsmouth, then rejoined Millwall.

1994 Ian Wright, Alan Smith and Kevin Campbell netted to give the Gunners a 3–1 Premiership win over Wimbledon at Selhurst Park.

9 October

1910   England international right-half Jack Crayston was born in Grange-over-Sands, Cumberland. He served Arsenal as both a player and a manager.

1948   Two goals by Reg Lewis plus another from Jimmy Logie gave the Gunners a 3–1 First Division win over Burnley at Highbury.

1971   George Graham, Ray Kennedy, George Armstrong and Eddie Kelly all registered in Arsenal's 4–2 victory over Newcastle United at Highbury.

1979   Strikes by Alan Sunderland and Graham Rix gave Terry Neill's side a 2–1 First Division win over Ipswich Town at Portman Road.

1990   Perry Groves scored twice as George Graham's side eased to a 5–0 Rumbelows League Cup second-round second-leg home win over Chester City.

10 October

1921   A charity rugby match between England and Australia to raise funds for the Russian Famine Fund was staged at Highbury.

1950   England international striker Charlie George, capped once as a Derby County player, was born in Islington, London. He became one of the most popular figures in Arsenal history.

1953   Two goals by Jimmy Logie plus others from Arthur Milton and Alex Forbes gave Arsenal a 4–1 First Division win at Tottenham Hotspur.

1966   England international central defender Tony Adams, who won 66 caps, was born in Romford, Essex. He scored 48 times in 659 outings for the Gunners between 1983/84 and 2001/02.

1987   Strikes by Paul Davis and Steve Williams gave George Graham's side a 2–0 First Division victory at home to Oxford United.

11 October

1919   Joe Toner made his League debut and Bert White scored twice in Arsenal's 3–2 victory over Everton at Goodison Park.

1958   Tottenham Hotspur celebrated Bill Nicholson's appointment as manager by trouncing Everton 10–4 at White Hart Lane.

1972   Arsenal central defender Jeff Blockley won his solitary cap for England in the 1–1 draw with Yugoslavia at Wembley.

1975   Alex Cropley and Brian Kidd netted two goals each as Arsenal cruised to a 5–0 First Division victory at home to Coventry City.

2000   Arsenal trio David Seaman, Ray Parlour and captain Martin Keown featured in England's 0–0 World Cup qualifier draw in Finland.

12 October

1884   England international winger Jock Rutherford, who earned 11 caps, was born in Percy Main, Northumberland. He scored 25 times in 222 League outings for the Gunners between 1913/14 and 1925/26.

1935   Jack Crayston scored to give George Allison's side a 1–1 First Division draw with Chelsea watched by 82,905 at Stamford Bridge.

1953   Two goals by Doug Lishman plus another from Tommy Lawton gave Arsenal a 3–1 win over Blackpool in the FA Charity Shield.

1991   Kenny Dalglish was appointed manager of Blackburn Rovers. He guided them to the Premiership title in 1994/95.

1996   Ian Wright scored both goals as the Gunners secured a 2–0 Premiership triumph over Blackburn Rovers at Ewood Park.

13 October

1928   England international David Jack cost a British record £10,890 from Bolton Wanderers as successor to the accomplished Charlie Buchan.

1960   Goalkeeper Jack McClelland was signed from Glenavon. He won five caps for Northern Ireland while at Highbury and moved to Fulham in 1964.

1971   Arsenal pair George Graham and Bob Wilson made their Scottish international debuts in the 2–1 win over Portugal at Hampden Park.

1984   Two goals by Brian Talbot plus others from Paul Mariner and Kenny Sansom gave Arsenal a 4–1 First Division win at Leicester City.

2001   For the first time in 16 years, Arsenal were without a member of the 'Famous Five' defenders – Lee Dixon, Tony Adams, Steve Bould, Nigel Winterburn and Martin Keown – in the 2–0 Premiership win at Southampton.

14 October

1893   Arthur Elliott netted a hat-trick as the Gunners stormed to a Club-record 12–0 FA Cup victory at home to Ashford United.

1989   Two goals by Perry Groves plus others from Paul Merson and Michael Thomas secured a 4–0 First Division win over Manchester City.

1995   Paul Merson, Dennis Bergkamp and Ian Wright registered in the Gunners' 3–0 Premiership win over Leeds United at Elland Road.

1997   Substitute Jehad Muntasser's one minute of first-team action came in the 4–1 Coca-Cola League Cup third-round win over Birmingham City. He is the only Libyan to have played for Arsenal.

2000   Thierry Henry's second-half strike gave Arsène Wenger's side a 1–0 Premiership victory over Aston Villa at Highbury.

15 October

1910   David Neave netted twice as George Morrell's team gained a 4–1 First Division victory at home to Blackburn Rovers.

1963   Late strikes by Joe Baker and Geoff Strong gave the Gunners a 4–4 First Division draw at home to Tottenham Hotspur.

1968   Arsenal triumphed 2–1 at home to Liverpool in the League Cup fourth round with goals from Peter Simpson and John Radford.

1973   Management duo Brian Clough and Peter Taylor resigned from Derby County. They later achieved success at Nottingham Forest.

1994   Two goals by Ian Wright plus another from Kevin Campbell gave the Gunners a 3–1 Premiership victory at home to Chelsea.

16 October

1919   Centre forward Fred Pagnam was signed from Liverpool. He topped Arsenal's League goalscoring chart with 14 goals in 1920/21.

1954   Arsenal full back Walley Barnes won his 22nd and last cap for Wales in the 1–0 defeat by Scotland in Cardiff.

1961   Striker Paul Vaessen was born in Bermondsey, London. The son of former Millwall and Gillingham wing-half Leon Vaessen, he netted nine goals in 41 outings for the Gunners, famously scoring against Juventus in the 1980 European Cup Winners' Cup semi final.

1999   England international Lee Dixon scored his first goal for three years in Arsenal's 4–1 Premiership victory over Everton at Highbury.

2004   Robert Pires netted twice as Arsenal stretched their unbeaten Premiership run to 49 games with a 3–1 win at home to Aston Villa. The record still stands today.

17 October

1925   Jimmy Brain grabbed a hat-trick as Herbert Chapman's team swept to a 5–0 First Division victory at home to Cardiff City.

1936   Long-serving Arsenal left half Bob John won his 15th and last cap for Wales in the 2–1 triumph over England in Cardiff.

1951   Doug Lishman scored twice as Arsenal won 3–2 in the first post-war friendly at home to Glasgow Rangers, watched by 62,012.

1973   England failed to qualify for the 1974 World Cup finals after being held to a 1–1 draw by Poland at Wembley Stadium.

2000   John Lukic, 39, became the oldest Gunner to play in the UEFA Champions League as Robert Pires' late equalizer clinched a 1–1 draw at Lazio and qualification for the next stage.

18 October

1933   Two goals by Ralph Birkett plus another from Ray Bowden gave Arsenal a 3–0 win over Everton in the FA Charity Shield.

1958   Arsenal forward David Herd made his Scotland international debut in the 3–0 victory over Wales in Cardiff.

1968   Scotland international winger Jimmy Robertson arrived from Tottenham Hotspur in an exchange deal involving Dave Jenkins.

2003   Strikes by Edu and Thierry Henry gave Arsenal a 2–1 Premiership win at home to Chelsea, the visitors' first defeat of the season.

2005   Thierry Henry became Arsenal's record goalscorer after a brace away to Sparta Prague in the UEFA Champions League surpassed Ian Wright's tally of 185.

19 October

1895   Peter Mortimer scored twice as the Gunners stormed to a 5–0 Second Division victory at home to Burton Swifts.

1929   Jack Lambert's hat-trick plus a goal from Joe Hulme gave Arsenal a 4–1 First Division win over Grimsby Town at Highbury.

1940   Alf Kirchen netted a hat-trick as the Gunners clinched a stirring 5–4 wartime South Regional League win over Northampton Town.

1991   David Rocastle scored as champions Arsenal held First Division leaders Manchester United to a 1–1 draw at Old Trafford.

1999   Dennis Bergkamp and Marc Overmars netted as Arsenal lost 4–2 to Barcelona in the UEFA Champions League Group B at Wembley.

20 October

1928   David Jack made his debut and Len Thompson scored twice in Arsenal's 3–0 First Division victory at Newcastle United.

1934   Ted Drake became the first Arsenal player to score a hat-trick against Tottenham Hotspur in a 5–1 First Division win at Highbury.

1958   Centre forward Cliff Holton moved from Arsenal to Watford. Thereafter he roamed the League, stopping off at Northampton Town, Crystal Palace, Watford again, Charlton Athletic and Orient.

1990   Anders Limpar scored in a 1–0 win at Manchester United but Arsenal were deducted two points, and United one, after a mass brawl during the game.

2001   Robert Pires, Dennis Bergkamp and Thierry Henry netted in Arsenal's 3–3 Premiership draw at home to Blackburn Rovers.

21 October

1961   Alan Skirton scored twice as George Swindin's team gained a thumping 5–1 First Division victory over Manchester United at Highbury.

1967   Arsenal centre half Ian Ure won his 11th and last cap for Scotland in the 1–0 defeat by Northern Ireland in Belfast.

1972   Goals by Charlie George, John Radford and Pat Rice secured a 3–2 First Division win over Crystal Palace at Selhurst Park.

1980   Brian Talbot, Brian McDermott and Kenny Sansom netted to earn Arsenal a 3–1 First Division victory at home to Norwich City.

2000   Robert Pires' strike plus Rio Ferdinand's own-goal gave joint leaders Arsenal a 2–1 Premiership win at West Ham United.

22 October

1949   Arsenal manager Arsène Wenger was born in Strasbourg, France. He master-minded the Gunners' 1997/98 and 2001/02 Double triumphs.

1960   Two goals by Geoff Strong plus others from Mel Charles and David Herd gave Arsenal a 4–2 First Division win at Blackburn Rovers.

1972   Stoke City and England goalkeeper Gordon Banks' illustrious playing career was ended when he lost an eye in a car crash.

1988   Three brothers – Danny, Rod and Ray Wallace – played for Southampton, the first such trio of brothers appearing in the top flight for 68 years.

2001   Former Arsenal manager Bertie Mee died, aged 82. He presided over the 1970 European Fairs Cup and 1970/71 Double successes during a ten-year reign.

23 October

1926 Jimmy Brain scored four goals and Samson Haden two in Arsenal's 6–2 First Division drubbing of Sheffield Wednesday at Highbury.

1935 Scotland international Neil Dewar's strike gave Sheffield Wednesday a 1–0 victory over Arsenal in the FA Charity Shield.

1948 Ronnie Rooke and Jimmy Logie netted two goals apiece in the Gunners' 5–0 First Division demolition of Everton at Highbury.

1957 England international midfielder Graham Rix was born in Mexborough, Yorkshire. He went on to play for Caen, Le Havre, Dundee and Chelsea.

1999 Kanu netted a late hat-trick as Arsenal came from two down to gain a 3–2 Premiership victory over Chelsea at Highbury.

24 October

1936 The East Stand at Highbury was opened for Arsenal's 0–0 draw with Grimsby Town. It seated 4,000 on each of its two tiers.

1953 Ben Marden grabbed a hat-trick as the Gunners swept to a 5–1 First Division victory over Charlton Athletic at The Valley.

1956 Long-serving Arsenal manager Tom Whittaker, 58, died of a heart attack at University College Hospital, London.

1974 Republic of Ireland international Terry Mancini joined from QPR. Previously he had played for Watford and Leyton Orient.

2004 Arsenal's unbeaten Premiership run ended at 49 matches in controversial circumstances as Manchester United triumphed 2–0 at Old Trafford.

25 October

1924   Jimmy Brain scored on his debut to clinch Arsenal's 1–0 First Division victory over Tottenham Hotspur at Highbury.

1955   England played the USA under floodlights in a Ladies international hockey match at Highbury.

1980   Pat Rice made his final appearance for Arsenal and Alan Sunderland's strike clinched the Gunners' 1–1 First Division draw at Liverpool.

1998   First-half goals from Nicolas Anelka and Emmanuel Petit gave Arsenal a 2–1 Premiership win over Blackburn Rovers at Ewood Park.

2000   Arsenal won 4–2 at home to Sparta Prague to secure top spot in the UEFA Champions League Group B and ensure being seeded.

26 October

1903   Tommy Shanks bagged a hat-trick and Tommy Pratt notched a brace as the Gunners hammered Leicester Fosse 8–0, their eighth straight win.

1932   Arsenal inside forward Alex James won his eighth and last cap for Scotland in the 3–2 victory over Wales in Edinburgh.

1938   Goals by Willie Hall, Tommy Lawton and Len Goulden gave England a 3–0 victory over Rest of Europe at Highbury.

1974   Terry Mancini made his debut as John Radford, Liam Brady and Brian Kidd scored in the 3–0 First Division win over West Ham United.

1996   Arsenal went top of the Premiership after Lee Dixon, Dennis Bergkamp and Ian Wright netted in the 3–0 victory over Leeds United.

27 October

1928   Len Thompson scored twice for the second consecutive match as Arsenal fought out an entertaining 4–4 First Division draw against Liverpool.

1952   A misleading report appeared in a Spanish newspaper mistaking as fact agency publicity for the *The Arsenal Stadium Mystery* film.

1962   Joe Baker scored a hat-trick and George Eastham contributed two goals in Arsenal's riveting 5–4 First Division win at home to Wolverhampton Wanderers.

1981   Willie Young scored on his final appearance in the 2–0 victory at home to Sheffield United in the Milk League Cup second-round second leg.

1987   Kevin Richardson, Alan Smith and Michael Thomas netted in Arsenal's 3–0 Littlewoods League Cup third-round win over AFC Bournemouth.

28 October

1936   Eddie Burbanks and Raich Carter scored to give Sunderland a 2–1 victory over George Allison's team in the FA Charity Shield.

1967   John Radford netted a hat-trick and Colin Addison chipped in with a brace in the Gunners' 5–3 First Division victory at home to Fulham.

1978   Two goals by Liam Brady plus another from Frank Stapleton gave Arsenal a 3–1 First Division win over Bristol City at Ashton Gate.

1986   David Rocastle, Martin Hayes and Paul Davis scored as Arsenal beat Manchester City 3–1 in the Littlewoods Cup third round.

2003   Cesc Fabregas became Arsenal's youngest first-team player at 16 years 177 days in the 1–1 draw with Rotherham Town.

29 October

1911   England international centre half Bernard Joy, who won a solitary cap, was born in Fulham. He made 86 First Division appearances while at Highbury.

1932   Joe Hulme netted a hat-trick and Cliff Bastin and Tim Coleman hit two goals each in the 8–2 First Division trouncing of Leicester City.

1965   Northern Ireland international full back Jimmy Magill joined Brighton and Hove Albion. He was a cultured performer who relied on stealth rather than strength.

1973   French international midfielder Robert Pires was born in Reims. He helped Arsenal to win the League title in 2001/02 and 2003/04 and the FA Cup in 2003 and 2005.

1983   Leading marksman Tony Woodcock scored five goals as Arsenal gained a 6–2 First Division victory at Aston Villa.

30 October

1897   Fergus Hunt grabbed a hat-trick as the Gunners galloped to a 9–0 FA Cup third-qualifying-round win at home to non-League St Albans.

1941   Scotland international goalkeeper Bob Wilson was born in Chesterfield. He was Player of the Year in Arsenal's 1970/71 Double season.

1985   Charlie Nicholas and Ian Allinson scored to give Arsenal a 2–1 Milk League Cup third-round win over Manchester City at Maine Road.

1990   Arsenal triumphed 2–1 at Manchester City in the Rumbelows League Cup third round with goals from Perry Groves and Tony Adams.

2004   Second-half goals by Thierry Henry and Robin van Persie gave leaders Arsenal a 2–2 Premiership draw at home to Southampton.

31 October

1925   Jimmy Brain's hat-trick plus a goal by Sid Hoar earned Arsenal a 4–1 First Division victory over Everton at Highbury.

1932   Arsenal gained a 5–2 friendly win at Racing Club de Paris with four goals by Cliff Bastin plus another from Jack Lambert.

1953   Cliff Holton and Jimmy Logie scored two goals apiece in the Gunners' 4–1 First Division victory at home to Sheffield Wednesday.

1959   David Herd, John Barnwell and Jackie Henderson netted in Arsenal's 3–0 First Division win over Birmingham City at Highbury.

1970   Eddie Kelly and John Radford scored in Arsenal's 2–0 First Division victory at home to Brian Clough's Derby County.

1 November

1913   Jock Rutherford scored twice on his debut as George Morrell's side gained a 3–2 Second Division win at home to Nottingham Forest.

1955   Arsenal midfielder John Matthews was born in Islington, London. He was a composed performer who could deputize in central defence if needed.

1969   John Radford's hat-trick plus goals by George Armstrong and George Graham gave Arsenal a comfortable 5–1 First Division win at Crystal Palace.

2000   Arsenal mourned the sudden death of long-serving former winger George Armstrong, 56, who held a coaching post at Highbury.

2003   Two goals by Thierry Henry plus others from Robert Pires and Gilberto Silva gave Arsenal a 4–1 Premiership win at Leeds United.

2 November

1907   Top scorer Peter Kyle netted twice as Phil Kelso's team secured a 5–1 First Division victory at home to Sheffield United.

1977   Striker Alan Sunderland was signed from Wolverhampton Wanderers, while midfielder Trevor Ross joined Everton.

1996   England Under-21 midfielder David Hillier moved to Portsmouth. He scored twice in 134 outings while at Highbury from 1990/01 to 1996/97.

1999   Two goals by Marc Overmars plus another from Davor Suker gave Arsenal a 3–2 UEFA Champions League win over AIK in Stockholm.

2005   Two goals by Robin van Persie plus another from Thierry Henry gave Arsenal a 3–0 win over Sparta Prague in the UEFA Champions League.

3 November

1951   Cliff Holton, Doug Lishman and Arthur Milton netted in Arsenal's 3–0 First Division victory over Middlesbrough at Ayresome Park.

1962   Joe Baker and Alan Skirton scored two goals each in the Gunners' remarkable 5–5 First Division draw with Blackburn Rovers at Ewood Park.

1963   England international striker and Arsenal superstar Ian Wright was born in Woolwich, London. He netted 184 goals in 287 outings for the Gunners between 1991/92 and 1997/98.

1971   Arsenal won 3–0 at home to Swiss side Grasshoppers in Zurich in the European Cup second-round second leg to triumph 5–0 on aggregate.

1993   Kevin Campbell scored twice in Arsenal's 7–0 UEFA Cup Winners' Cup second-round second-leg win at Standard Liege, their biggest win in Europe.

4 November

1931   England Under-23 centre half Bill Dodgin was born in Wardley Colliery, County Durham. After leaving Arsenal he played for Fulham, then managed several clubs.

1937   Welsh international inside forward Les Jones joined Arsenal from Coventry City in an exchange deal involving Bobby Davidson.

1955   Full back Stan Charlton and forward Vic Groves signed for the Gunners from Leyton Orient in a joint transfer package.

1978   Frank Stapleton's hat-trick plus a goal by Sammy Nelson gave Arsenal a 4–1 First Division win at home to Ipswich Town.

1989   Norwich City led by three goals before Arsenal fought back and Lee Dixon's last-gasp penalty clinched a 4–3 First Division win.

5 November

1909   England international goalkeeper Frank Moss was born in Leyland, Lancashire. He featured in three successive League Championship triumphs in 1932/33, 1933/34 and 1934/35.

1932   Herbert Chapman persuaded London Electric Railway to change the name of the station Gillespie Road to Arsenal, and it is still the only London Underground station named after a football club.

1937   England international Ray Bowden joined Newcastle United. He once scored more than 100 goals in a season for his local club, Looe.

1952   Arsenal inside forward Jimmy Logie made his sole international appearance for Scotland in the 1–1 draw with Northern Ireland at Hampden Park.

2003   Ashley Cole's late strike fuelled Arsenal's hopes with a 1–0 victory at home to Dynamo Kiev in the UEFA Champions League Group B.

6 November

1964 England Under-21 midfielder Stewart Robson was born in Billericay, Essex. He was voted Arsenal's Player of the Year in 1985, but in 1987 he joined his boyhood favourites, West Ham United.

1965 Joe Baker, Alan Skirton and George Armstrong scored two goals each in Arsenal's 6–2 First Division win over Sheffield United.

1968 Arsenal left-back Bob McNab won the first of his four caps for England in the 0–0 draw with Romania in Bucharest.

1976 Frank Stapleton, Sammy Nelson, Malcolm Macdonald and Trevor Ross all netted in the 4–0 First Division home win over Birmingham City.

1988 Arsenal gained a 4–1 First Division win at Nottingham Forest with goals by Alan Smith, Steve Bould, Tony Adams and Brian Marwood.

7 November

1901 Centre forward Billy Gooing was signed from Chesterfield. He netted 45 goals in 94 League outings for the Gunners between 1901 and 1905.

1913 Goalkeeper Hugh McDonald moved to Fulham. He made a total of 94 League appearances during three spells with the Gunners.

1925 John Robson made his final appearance and Jimmy Brain scored twice in Arsenal's 5–2 First Division win at Manchester City.

1964 Prolific inside forward Geoff Strong was sold to Liverpool. At Anfield he became a top utility player, winning League title and FA Cup medals.

1992 Arsenal went top of the Premier League after Alan Smith, Ian Wright and Kevin Campbell scored in a 3–0 win over Coventry City.

8 November

1924   Centre forward Bobby Turnbull moved to Charlton Athletic. He netted 26 goals in 59 First Division games for the Gunners.

1927   Long-serving full back Len Wills was born in Hackney, north London. He scored four times in 208 outings during a Highbury stint from 1953/54 to 1960/61.

1932   Much-travelled winger Gordon Nutt, who also played for Coventry City, Cardiff City, Southend United and PSV Eindhoven, was born in Birmingham. He netted ten goals in 49 First Division outings for Arsenal.

1980   John Hollins scored twice as Terry Neill's team swept to a 5–0 First Division victory over Leeds United at Elland Road.

1999   Arsenal defeated Real Madrid 3–1 at Highbury in a testimonial match for England international right back Lee Dixon.

9 November

1925   Scotland international goalkeeper Bill Harper, who won 11 caps, joined from Hibernian. He made 63 League appearances during two spells at Highbury.

1938   Arsenal inside forward Les Jones scored his only international goal in his 11th and last appearance for Wales in the 3–2 defeat by Scotland.

1974   Two goals by Alan Ball plus another from Liam Brady gave Arsenal a 3–1 First Division win over leaders Liverpool at Anfield

1997   Nicolas Anelka scored his first goal for Arsenal in a 3–2 Premiership victory over title rivals Manchester United at Highbury.

2004   Arturo Lupoli registered twice as a young Arsenal side came from behind to win 3–1 at home to Everton in the Carling Cup fourth round.

10 November

1951   Doug Lishman scored a hat-trick and Cliff Holton notched twice in Arsenal's entertaining 6–3 First Division win at home to West Bromwich Albion.

1959   Midfielder Peter Nicholas was born in Newport. When he arrived at Highbury in March 1981, he helped to transform the Gunners' fortunes as they rose from mid-table to claim a place in Europe.

1961   Centre half Allan Young moved from Arsenal to Chelsea. He made four First Division appearances during a brief career at Highbury.

1969   German international goalkeeper Jens Lehmann was born in Essen. He was ever-present during Arsenal's 2003/04 Premiership title-winning campaign.

1993   Two goals by Ian Wright plus another from Paul Merson earned Arsenal a 3–0 win at Norwich City in a Coca-Cola Cup third-round replay.

11 November

1930   Jack Lambert scored four times as Arsenal beat Racing Club Paris 7–2 in an Armistice Day friendly at Colombes Stadium.

1950   Four goals by Doug Lishman plus another from Don Roper gave Arsenal a 5–1 First Division win over Sunderland at Highbury.

1970   French central defender Gilles Grimandi was born in Gap. He netted four goals in 114 Premiership outings while at Highbury.

1972   Two goals by John Radford plus another from Peter Marinello gave Arsenal a 3–1 First Division victory at Wolverhampton Wanderers.

1989   Strikes from Niall Quinn and Michael Thomas earned George Graham's side a 2–1 First Division win over Millwall at The Den.

12 November

1921   Jimmy Hopkins netted twice as Leslie Knighton's team swept to a 5–2 First Division victory over Birmingham at Highbury.

1927   Arsenal gained a 3–1 First Division win at home to Middlesbrough with two goals by Charlie Buchan plus another from Joe Hulme.

1949   Goals from Jimmy Logie and Freddie Cox secured Tom Whittaker's side a 2–0 First Division victory at Manchester City.

1955   Vic Groves scored on his debut and another goal by Don Roper clinched Arsenal's 2–1 First Division win over Sheffield United.

1988   Steve Bould registered for the second consecutive match in the 1–0 First Division victory over Newcastle United at St James' Park.

13 November

1920   Goals from Bert White and Fred Pagnam gave Leslie Knighton's team a 2–0 First Division win at home to Blackburn Rovers.

1926   Billy Blyth, Samson Haden and Jimmy Ramsay registered in Arsenal's 3–3 First Division draw with Huddersfield Town at Leeds Road.

1979   Frank Stapleton and Paul Vaessen scored two goals apiece in Arsenal's 4–0 League Cup fourth-round replay victory over Brighton and Hove Albion.

1996   Ian Wright hit two goals as Arsenal came from behind to win 5–2 at home to Stoke City in a Coca-Cola League Cup third-round replay.

2004   Thierry Henry, Lauren, Patrick Vieira, Freddie Ljungberg and Robert Pires all scored in Arsenal's 5–4 Premiership win at Tottenham Hotspur, a stunning contest which featured the most goals ever in a north London derby.

14 November

1914 Leading marksman Harry King scored twice in the Gunners' 6–0 Second Division slamming of Grimsby Town at Highbury.

1925 Goalkeeper Bill Harper made his debut as Jimmy Brain netted a hat-trick in Arsenal's 6–1 First Division win at home to Bury.

1934 Seven Arsenal players featured in England's 3–2 victory over Italy, dubbed 'The Battle of Highbury'. No club has ever supplied more men for an England game.

1953 Cliff Holton's hat-trick plus a goal from Doug Lishman gave Arsenal a 4–3 First Division win at home to Bolton Wanderers.

1987 David Rocastle netted twice as leaders Arsenal gained their tenth successive First Division victory, 4–2 away to Norwich City.

15 November

1924 Goalkeeper Dan Lewis made his debut as Jimmy Ramsay scored twice in Arsenal's 3–2 First Division victory at Everton.

1950 Arsenal centre half Leslie Compton became the oldest debutant for England, at 38 years 64 days, in the 4–2 victory over Wales.

1951 Arsenal left back Lionel Smith won the first of his six caps for England in the 4–2 victory over Wales at Ninian Park.

1952 Cliff Holton netted a hat-trick and Ben Marden added two goals in Arsenal's 5–1 First Division drubbing of Liverpool at Anfield.

1986 Martin Hayes, Niall Quinn, Perry Groves and Viv Anderson all scored in the Gunners' 4–0 First Division win away to Southampton.

16 November

1938 Tottenham Hotspur inside forward Willie Hall scored a record five goals in England's 7–0 victory over Northern Ireland.

1957 Arsenal gained a 3–2 First Division victory at home to Portsmouth with two goals by David Herd plus another from Danny Clapton.

1962 England central defender Steve Bould was born in Stoke-on-Trent. After leaving the Gunners he played for Sunderland before returning to Highbury as a coach.

1974 Alan Ball scored twice for the second consecutive match as Arsenal gained a 3–1 First Division win at home to Derby County.

2002 Arsenal returned to the top of the Premiership as Thierry Henry scored a brilliant solo goal in a 3–0 win over Tottenham Hotspur at Highbury.

17 November

1961 England international wing-half Eddie Clamp arrived from Wolverhampton Wanderers. He helped to lift two League titles and the FA Cup during his Molineux days.

1980 Northern Ireland international Pat Rice joined Watford. He later returned to Highbury as a coach, then became Arsène Wenger's number two.

1990 Arsenal kept their sixth consecutive clean sheet as Alan Smith scored twice in a 4–0 First Division victory at home to Southampton.

1993 Arsenal striker Ian Wright found the net four times as England stormed to a 7–1 World Cup qualifier win over San Marino in Bologna. However it wasn't enough to see them qualify for the 1994 Wold Cup.

2001 Robert Pires' goal earned Arsenal a 1–1 Premiership draw at Tottenham Hotspur, the England defender's former club.

18 November

1931   Arsenal winger Cliff Bastin gained the first of his 21 caps for England in the 3–1 victory over Wales at Anfield.

1950   Goals by Doug Lishman, Jimmy Logie and Don Roper gave the Gunners a 3–1 First Division win over Liverpool at Anfield.

1960   Gifted inside forward George Eastham joined Arsenal from Newcastle United after protracted transfer negotiations.

1989   Lee Dixon, Alan Smith and Siggi Jonsson registered as George Graham's team secured a 3–0 First Division win at home to QPR.

2002   Arsenal midfielder Freddie Ljungberg was named Swedish Footballer of the Year. He starred in the Gunners' 2001/02 Double success, also pocketing medals for a League title in 2003/04 and FA Cup-winning gongs for 2003 and 2005.

19 November

1897   England right back Tom Parker was born in Woolston, Hampshire. He captained Arsenal to FA Cup Final triumph against Huddersfield Town in 1930.

1929   Welsh international goalkeeper Jack Kelsey, who won 41 caps, was born in Llansamlet, Swansea. He made 327 First Division appearances for the Gunners.

1960   England Under-23 inside forward Jimmy Bloomfield joined Birmingham City. After a steady stint at St Andrews he served Brentford, West Ham United, Plymouth Argyle and Orient.

1977   Arsenal gained a 2–1 First Division victory at Newcastle United with goals from Frank Stapleton and Alan Sunderland.

1988   Two goals by Paul Merson plus another from David Rocastle gave Arsenal a 3–0 First Division win at home to Middlesbrough.

20 November

1948 Skipper Joe Mercer scored his first own-goal in 18 years, in Arsenal's 1–0 First Division defeat at home to Newcastle United.

1963 England's 8–3 defeat of Northern Ireland was the first international at Wembley to be played entirely under floodlights.

1968 John Radford scored to give Bertie Mee's team a 1–0 victory at home to Tottenham Hotspur in the League Cup semi-final first leg (see 4 December, page 177, for second leg).

1971 Ted MacDougall scored a record nine goals in Bournemouth's 11–0 FA Cup first-round victory over Margate at Dean Court.

1999 Marc Overmars plundered a hat-trick and Dennis Bergkamp hit a brace in the 5–1 Premiership mauling of Middlesbrough at Highbury.

21 November

1903 Tommy Shanks netted twice as the promotion-chasing Gunners charged to a 6–0 Second Division win at home to Chesterfield.

1945 Stanley Matthews and Stan Mortensen guested for Arsenal in the 4–3 defeat by Moscow Dynamo at foggy White Hart Lane.

1959 Two goals by Joe Haverty plus another from Jimmy Bloomfield gave Arsenal a 3–1 First Division win over Chelsea at Stamford Bridge.

1962 England striker Alan Smith, who was capped 13 times, was born in Birmingham. He netted 115 goals in 345 outings for the Gunners between 1987/88 and 1994/95.

1995 Dennis Bergkamp, Nigel Winterburn, Paul Dickov and John Hartson all registered in the 4–2 Premiership win over Sheffield Wednesday.

22 November

1924   Leslie Knighton signed Luton Town winger Sid Hoar. He netted 16 goals in 100 First Division games for Arsenal.

1930   Jack Lambert scored a hat-trick and Cliff Bastin contributed two goals in Arsenal's 5–3 First Division victory at home to Middlesbrough.

1962   Arsenal striker Raphael Meade was born in Islington, London. He scored 14 times in 41 First Division outings while at Highbury.

2003   Arsenal broke Liverpool's unbeaten Premiership record from the start of the season, winning 3–0 at Birmingham City in their 13th match.

2005   Substitute Robert Pires netted a late penalty to clinch Arsenal's 1–0 UEFA Champions League victory over FC Thun in Switzerland.

23 November

1919   Scotland international inside forward Jimmy Logie was born in Edinburgh. He helped Arsenal to two League titles, in 1947/48 and 1952/53.

1935   Two goals by Ted Drake plus others from Tim Rogers and Joe Hulme secured a 4–0 First Division win over Wolverhampton Wanderers at Highbury.

1938   Scotland international winger Johnny MacLeod was born in Edinburgh. Arsenal boss George Swindin saw his 1961 purchase as a coup, but he didn't thrive under new manager Billy Wright.

1963   Jim Furnell made his debut on his 26th birthday as Geoff Strong scored twice in Arsenal's 5–3 First Division win over Blackpool.

1982   Alan Sunderland grabbed a hat-trick as Arsenal gained a 3–0 Milk Cup third-round replay victory over Everton at Highbury.

24 November

1895   Scottish wing-half Billy Milne was born in Buckie, Banffshire. He scored once in 114 League games for Arsenal, then was trainer for 33 years.

1934   Four goals by Ted Drake plus another from Joe Hulme gave the Gunners a 5–2 First Division win over Chelsea at Stamford Bridge.

1951   Doug Lishman netted a hat-trick against Bolton Wanderers after fluorescent sightscreens made the goals more visible in dense smog.

1996   Late strikes by Tony Adams and Dennis Bergkamp clinched Arsenal's 3–1 Premiership win over Tottenham Hotspur at Highbury.

2004   Despite the dismissal of Lauren and Patrick Vieira, Arsenal gained a 1–1 draw at PSV Eindhoven in the UEFA Champions League Group E.

25 November

1951   Scotland Under-23 central defender Willie Young was born in Edinburgh. He played for Arsenal in three successive FA Cup finals between 1978 and 1980.

1953   England lost 6–3 to Hungary at Wembley as the Olympic champions ended their unbeaten home record against foreign opposition.

1998   UEFA Champions League hopes ended after Arsenal lost 1–0 to Lens watched by a record 'home' crowd of 73,707 at Wembley Stadium.

2001   Two goals by Thierry Henry plus another from Freddie Ljungberg earned Arsenal a 3–1 Premiership win over Manchester United.

2003   Ace marksman Thierry Henry scored twice as Arsenal gained a thrilling 5–1 UEFA Champions League victory over Inter Milan in Italy.

26 November

1932   Two goals by Tim Coleman plus others from Joe Hulme and David Jack gave Arsenal a 4–2 First Division win over Middlesbrough.

1958   Arsenal winger Danny Clapton made his only international appearance for England in the 2–2 draw with Wales at Villa Park.

1960   David Herd grabbed a hat-trick as George Swindin's side gained a 3–2 First Division victory over Everton at Highbury.

1969   George Graham scored twice in the Gunners' 3–0 win at home to Sporting Lisbon in the European Fairs Cup second-round second leg.

1985   Martin Hayes, Charlie Nicholas and Stewart Robson registered in Arsenal's 3–1 Milk Cup fourth-round replay win at Southampton.

27 November

1926   Arsenal gained a 3–1 First Division win at West Bromwich Albion with goals by Joe Hulme, Samson Haden and Jimmy Brain.

1937   Two goals by Ted Drake plus others from Cliff Bastin and Alf Kirchen secured Arsenal a 4–1 First Division win over Leeds United.

1971   Strikes by Eddie Kelly and John Radford earned the Gunners a 2–1 First Division victory over Crystal Palace at Highbury.

1976   Terry Neill's team completed a 2–1 First Division victory at Coventry City with goals by Malcolm Macdonald and Frank Stapleton.

2002   Thierry Henry scored a stunning hat-trick as Arsenal came from behind to triumph 3–1 at Roma in the UEFA Champions League.

28 November

1931   Jack Lambert scored a hat-trick and David Jack scored two goals in Arsenal's 6–0 First Division demolition of Liverpool at Highbury.

1934   Ralph Birkett, Cliff Bastin, Ted Drake and Dr James Marshall all netted in Arsenal's 4–0 win over Manchester City in the FA Charity Shield.

1951   Gloucestershire and England cricketer Arthur Milton made his only footballing appearance for his country in the 2–2 draw with Austria at Wembley.

1955   Floodlights were used for the first time in the FA Cup as Darlington beat Carlisle United 3–1 in a first-round second replay at St James' Park.

1990   Manchester United stunned Arsenal as Lee Sharpe netted a hat-trick in the Red Devils' 6–2 Rumbelows Cup fourth-round win at Highbury.

29 November

1896   Arsenal right back Joe Powell, 26, died of blood poisoning and tetanus after breaking his arm during a match six days earlier.

1946   England left half Joe Mercer arrived from Everton. He earned five caps while with the Toffees before the war, then scored four goals for the Gunners in 247 League games between 1946/47 and 1953/54.

1978   Viv Anderson became the first black player to appear for England in a full international in the 1–0 win over Czechoslovakia at Wembley.

1983   Ian Allinson made his Arsenal debut as goals by Mark Rees and Ally Brown gave Walsall a shock 2–1 Milk Cup fourth-round win at Highbury.

1995   Strikes by Ian Wright and John Hartson earned Arsenal a 2–1 Coca-Cola Cup fourth-round victory at home to Sheffield Wednesday.

30 November

1944   Scotland international George Graham was born in Bargeddie, Lanarkshire. He played a prominent role in Arsenal's 1970/71 Double success and later returned as manager.

1983   Former England Schoolboys' captain and Under-21 central defender Tommy Caton arrived from Manchester City.

1994   Vince Bartram made his debut as substitute goalkeeper as Arsenal beat Sheffield Wednesday 2–0 in the Coca-Cola Cup fourth round.

1999   Arsenal lost 3–1 on penalties to Middlesbrough after a 2–2 draw at Riverside Stadium in the Worthington League Cup fourth round.

2002   Two goals by Thierry Henry plus another from Robert Pires gave leaders Arsenal a 3–1 Premiership victory over Aston Villa at Highbury.

1 December

1934   Ted Drake scored four goals and Ralph Birkett struck twice in Arsenal's 7–0 First Division rampage at home to Wolverhampton Wanderers.

1962   Two goals by Johnny MacLeod plus others from Joe Baker and Geoff Strong gave Arsenal a 4–2 First Division win at Manchester City.

1984   Ian Allinson, Tony Woodcock and Viv Anderson netted in the Gunners' 3–1 First Division triumph over Luton Town at Highbury.

1999   Arsenal striker Kanu was named African Footballer of the Year. The Nigerian international had joined the Gunners from Internazionale of Milan earlier in the year.

2001   Goals from Freddie Ljungberg and Thierry Henry gave Arsène Wenger's side a 2–0 Premiership victory at Ipswich Town.

2 December

1907 The PFA held its inaugural meeting, chaired by Manchester United star Billy Meredith at the Imperial Hotel, Manchester.

1967 Arsenal pair Frank McLintock and Peter Storey were sent off during the 1–0 First Division defeat by Burnley at Turf Moor.

1970 Ray Kennedy scored twice as holders Arsenal gained a 4–0 European Fairs Cup third-round first-leg victory at home to Belgian side Beveren-Waas.

1990 Goals from Paul Merson, Lee Dixon and Alan Smith earned leaders Arsenal a 3–0 First Division win over Liverpool at Highbury.

2003 Cesc Fabregas became the club's youngest goalscorer at just 16 as Arsenal beat Wolverhampton Wanderers 5–1 in the Carling Cup fourth round.

3 December

1898 Billy White scored a hat-trick and David Hannah netted two goals in the Gunners' 5–1 Second Division win at home to Newton Heath, later to become Manchester United.

1932 Two goals by Cliff Bastin plus another from David Jack gave title-chasing Arsenal a 3–1 First Division victory at Portsmouth.

1938 Ted Drake, Jack Crayston and Dave Nelson registered to give George Allison's team a 3–1 First Division win over Birmingham City.

1989 George Graham's side clinched a 1–0 First Division victory at home to Manchester United with a goal from Perry Groves.

1994 Strikes by Martin Keown and Paul Davis secured a 2–2 Premiership draw against Nottingham Forest at the City Ground.

4 December

1914   Goalkeeper George Swindin was born in Campsall, Yorkshire. He made 271 League appearances for Arsenal between 1936/37 and 1953/54, then returned as manager for four years from 1958.

1968   Arsenal reached Wembley after a 1–1 draw at Tottenham Hotspur in the League Cup semi-final second leg clinched a 2–1 aggregate win.

1974   Scotland international midfielder Alex Cropley arrived from Hibernian. He scored six times in 34 games for Arsenal before leaving to join Aston Villa in 1976.

1991   Arsenal's former England international winger Cliff Bastin, 79, died in Exeter. He held the club's goalscoring record at the time.

2001   Two goals by Freddie Ljungberg plus another from Thierry Henry gave Arsenal a 3–1 win over Juventus in the UEFA Champions League.

5 December

1904   Bob Watson netted seven goals in the Gunners' incredible 26–1 friendly win over Paris XI, effectively the French national team.

1964   Two goals by Joe Baker and strikes by Alan Skirton and George Armstrong saw Arsenal claim both points with a thrilling 4–3 First Division win at Fulham.

1967   John Radford and Terry Neill scored to give Bertie Mee's side a 2–1 League Cup fifth-round replay victory at home to Burnley.

1981   Stewart Robson made his debut and goals from John Hollins and Chris Whyte secured a 2–1 First Division win at West Ham United.

1987   Perry Groves, Kevin Richardson and Paul Merson were on target in Arsenal's 3–1 First Division victory at home to Sheffield Wednesday.

6 December

1924 Harry Woods' hat-trick plus a goal from Joe Toner earned the Gunners a 4–0 First Division win over Preston North End at Highbury.

1955 England international striker Tony Woodcock was born in Nottingham. He was Arsenal's leading marksman in four successive seasons from 1982/83 to 1985/86.

1969 Strikes by Jon Sammels and John Radford gave Bertie Mee's team a 2–2 First Division draw with Southampton at Highbury.

1986 Two goals by Martin Hayes plus another from Niall Quinn secured George Graham's team a 3–1 First Division win at home to QPR.

1997 Ian Wright's first-half strike clinched Arsenal's 1–0 Premiership victory over Newcastle United at St James' Park.

7 December

1911 Centre forward Ronnie Rooke was born in Guildford, Surrey. He was top scorer in Arsenal's 1947/48 League title success with 33 goals.

1932 Arsenal inside forward David Jack won his ninth and last cap for England in the 4–3 victory over Austria at Stamford Bridge.

1939 Scotland centre half Ian Ure was born in Ayr. Before joining the Gunners he had helped Dundee to reach the European Cup semi-finals.

1968 John Radford, David Court and George Graham scored in Arsenal's 3–1 First Division win over Everton at Goodison Park.

2002 Arsenal lost 2–0 at Manchester United after scoring in 55 consecutive League matches to beat the record, 47, set by Chesterfield in 1930.

8 December

1925 Arsenal centre half Jack Butler made his only international appearance for England in the 4–0 win over Belgium at The Hawthorns.

1926 Centre half Herbie Roberts joined Arsenal from non-League Oswestry Town. He helped the Gunners to win four League titles in the 1930s.

1928 Two goals by David Jack plus another from Jimmy Brain gave Arsenal a 3–1 First Division win over Manchester United.

1979 Frank Stapleton, Alan Sunderland and David O'Leary netted in Arsenal's 3–1 First Division victory over Coventry City.

2002 Arsène Wenger was Coach of the Year in the BBC Sports Personality awards after guiding the Gunners to their Double triumph in 2001/02.

9 December

1961 England Under-21 midfielder Paul Davis was born in Dulwich, London. He scored 37 times in 445 outings while at Highbury.

1981 Scotland Under-23 central defender Willie Young joined Nottingham Forest. He had started his career at Aberdeen, then served Tottenham Hotspur before arriving at Highbury.

1998 Alberto Mendez, Nicolas Anelka and Luis Boa Morte scored as Arsenal's makeshift team won 3–1 at Panathinaikos in the UEFA Champions League.

1999 Goals by Gilles Grimandi, Thierry Henry and Marc Overmars secured a 3–3 draw at Nantes in the UEFA Cup-third round second leg.

2000 Ray Parlour's superb hat-trick plus goals by Thierry Henry and Kanu gave Arsenal a memorable 5–0 Premiership win at home to Newcastle United.

10 December

1926   Herbert Chapman signed Notts County left back Horace Cope, who missed the 1927 FA Cup Final defeat by Cardiff City because of a knee injury.

1932   The West Stand at Highbury was officially opened by HRH Prince of Wales before the 4–1 First Division win at home to Chelsea.

1960   George Eastham scored twice on his debut as Arsenal gained a 5–1 First Division victory over Bolton Wanderers at Highbury.

1963   Joe Baker and George Eastham netted two goals apiece in the Gunners' comprehensive 6–0 First Division victory at home to Everton.

2003   Strikes by Robert Pires and Freddie Ljungberg gave Arsenal a 2–0 win over Lokomotiv Moscow in the UEFA Champions League.

11 December

1886   The Club, then known as Dial Square, trounced Eastern Wanderers 6–0 in their first ever match, a friendly on the Isle of Dogs.

1909   Bill Buckenham and David Neave scored two goals apiece as the Gunners gained a 4–3 First Division win at Preston North End.

1954   Two goals by Don Roper plus another from Arthur Milton earned Arsenal a 3–1 First Division win over Charlton Athletic.

1960   England Under-21 goalkeeper John Lukic was born in Chesterfield. He made 297 appearances during two successful spells at Highbury, from 1983/84 to 1989/90 and 1996/97 to 2000/01.

1963   England left back Nigel Winterburn was born in Nuneaton, Warwickshire. He accumulated seven major club honours during a glorious Arsenal career.

12 December

1896   Arsenal crashed to a record 8–0 League defeat at Loughborough, while the reserves won 5–0 at home to Leyton in the FA Cup.

1936   Four goals by Bobby Davidson plus another from Ted Drake gave Arsenal a 5–1 First Division victory at Portsmouth.

1946   Centre forward Ronnie Rooke joined Arsenal from Fulham with Dave Nelson and Cyril Grant moving in the opposite direction.

1991   Twice-capped England midfielder Michael Thomas moved to Liverpool. Having helped the Gunners pip the Merseysiders to the title in 1988/89, he netted for his new employers in their FA Cup Final victory of 1992.

2004   Thierry Henry scored twice but Chelsea twice cancelled out Arsenal's lead as the top-of-the-table clash ended 2–2 at Highbury.

13 December

1930   David Jack scored to give Herbert Chapman's title-chasing side a 1–1 First Division draw against Liverpool at Anfield.

1947   Two goals by Ronnie Rooke plus others from Jimmy Logie and Don Roper earned Arsenal a 4–0 First Division win at Grimsby Town.

1969   Jimmy Robertson, John Radford and George Armstrong scored in the Gunners' 3–2 First Division victory at home to Burnley.

1976   England midfielder Alan Hudson, who received two caps, arrived from Stoke City, while John Radford left Arsenal to join West Ham United.

1999   Gilles Grimandi, Tony Adams and Marc Overmars netted in Arsenal's 3–1 FA Cup third-round win over Blackpool at Highbury.

14 December

1922   England B international forward Don Roper was born in Botley, Hampshire. He helped Arsenal win two League titles, in 1947/48 and 1952/53.

1935   Ted Drake plundered a sensational Club-record seven goals in Arsenal's 7–1 First Division victory over Aston Villa at Villa Park.

1937   Winger Jackie Milne was sold to Middlesbrough. He gained Scotland international recognition while at Ayresome Park.

1957   Strikes by Gordon Nutt, David Herd and Jimmy Bloomfield plus Joe Dunn's own-goal secured a 4–2 First Division win over Preston North End.

2003   Arsenal returned to the top of the Premiership after Dennis Bergkamp's goal clinched a 1–0 victory at home to Blackburn Rovers.

15 December

1934   Ted Drake and Joe Hulme banged in hat-tricks as Arsenal stormed to an 8–0 First Division victory at home to Leicester City.

1951   Two goals by Don Roper plus another from Reg Lewis gave the Gunners a 3–2 First Division win at Huddersfield Town.

1956   Arsenal gained a 3–2 First Division victory at Cardiff City with two goals by David Herd plus another from Joe Haverty.

1984   Ian Allinson scored twice as Don Howe's side secured a 4–0 First Division victory at home to West Bromwich Albion.

2002   Robert Pires' penalty equalizer just before half time gave leaders Arsenal a 1–1 Premiership draw at Tottenham Hotspur.

16 December

1905   Phil Kelso signed winger Billy Garbutt from Reading. He netted eight goals in 52 First Division outings for the Gunners.

1911   Two goals by John Chalmers plus another from Charlie Randall secured a 3–1 First Division win at home to Middlesbrough.

1961   Arsenal gained a 2–0 First Division triumph over high-flying Burnley at Turf Moor with goals from Alan Skirton and Mel Charles.

1978   Strikes by David Price and Frank Stapleton gave Terry Neill's side a 2–0 First Division win over Derby County at Highbury.

1989   Alan Smith, Brian Marwood and Paul Merson scored in Arsenal's 3–2 First Division victory at home to Luton Town.

17 December

1904   Tom Fitchie snatched a hat-trick and Charlie Satterthwaite hit a brace in the Gunners' 5–1 First Division win at Notts County.

1938   Two goals by Reg Lewis plus others from Cliff Bastin and George Drury gave Arsenal a 4–1 First Division win over Stoke City.

1944   Scotland international winger Jimmy Robertson, capped only once, was born in Glasgow. He netted eight goals in 59 games for Arsenal in 1968/69 and 1969/70.

1955   Dennis Evans, hearing a whistle from the crowd, thought it was full time and scored an own-goal in Arsenal's 4–1 win over Blackpool.

1983   Raphael Meade grabbed a hat-trick as the Gunners secured a 3–1 First Division victory over Watford at Highbury.

18 December

1948   Ronnie Rooke netted a hat-trick as Tom Whittaker's side earned a 3–0 First
Division win at home to Huddersfield Town.

1954   The only instance of a 'shared own-goal' by Stan Milburn and Jack Froggatt
came in Leicester City's 3–1 defeat at Chelsea.

1971   John Roberts scored both goals in Arsenal's 2–0 First Division victory at home
to Don Howe's West Bromwich Albion.

1976   Two goals by Malcolm Macdonald plus another from Liam Brady secured a 3–1
First Division win over Manchester United.

2000   Patrick Vieira's late equalizer gave Arsenal a 1–1 Premiership draw against
Tottenham Hotspur at White Hart Lane.

19 December

1903   Four goals by Tommy Shanks plus another from Tim Coleman earned the
Gunners a 5–1 Second Division win over Grimsby Town.

1912   England marksman Alf Common, who averaged a goal a game from his three
international outings, moved from Arsenal to Preston North End.

1931   David Jack and Cliff Bastin scored two goals apiece in Arsenal's 5–2 First
Division win over Middlesbrough at Ayresome Park.

1970   Frank McLintock, George Graham and Ray Kennedy netted in the Gunners' 3–1
First Division victory at Manchester United.

2004   Sol Campbell scored his only goal of the season to clinch Arsenal's 1–0
Premiership victory over Portsmouth at Fratton Park.

20 December

1924 Four goals by Jimmy Brain plus others from Harry Woods and Jimmy Ramsay gave Arsenal an easy 6–1 First Division win over Leeds United.

1952 Doug Lishman, Cliff Holton and Don Roper scored to give the Gunners a 3–1 First Division victory at home to Aston Villa.

1980 England left back Ashley Cole was born in Stepney, London. He was a key figure in Arsenal's 2001/02 Double success and in subsequent triumphs.

1986 Goals by Niall Quinn, Tony Adams and Martin Hayes secured Arsenal a 3–0 First Division victory at home to Luton Town.

1998 Gilles Grimandi was sent off but Dennis Bergkamp, Patrick Vieira and Emmanuel Petit scored in the 3–1 Premiership win over Leeds United.

21 December

1957 Two goals by David Herd plus another from Vic Groves saw the Gunners to a 3–0 First Division win at home to Sunderland.

1957 Johnny Summers scored five goals in Charlton Athletic's remarkable 7–6 Second Division win at home to Huddersfield Town.

1985 Gus Caesar made his League debut and Charlie Nicholas' goal clinched Arsenal's 1–0 First Division win at Manchester United.

1991 Ian Wright, returning from injury, scored four times in the Gunners' 4–2 First Division victory at Manchester United.

2005 Arsène Wenger's young side defeated Doncaster Rovers 3–1 on penalties after a 2–2 Carling League Cup fifth-round draw at Belle Vue.

22 December

1928   Arsenal gained a 3–1 First Division win at home to Burnley with goals from Joe Hulme, Harry Peel and Jimmy Brain.

1956   Johnny Watts netted an own-goal as Jack Crayston's team swept to a 4–0 First Division victory over Birmingham City.

1962   Arsenal were leading 1–0 at Manchester United when the First Division match was abandoned after 57 minutes due to fog.

1971   England's World Cup-winning midfielder Alan Ball, who accumulated 72 caps, arrived from Everton. He was Arsenal's Player of the Year in 1973/74.

1996   Former England goalkeeper Peter Shilton made his 1,000th League appearance in Leyton Orient's 2–0 win at home to Brighton.

23 December

1967   Two goals by George Graham plus another from George Armstrong earned Arsenal a 3–0 First Division win over Nottingham Forest.

1976   Midfield dynamo Alan Ball joined Southampton. Later he embarked on a varied management career with Blackpool, his first professional club.

1978   Alan Sunderland's hat-trick plus goals by Frank Stapleton and Liam Brady secured a 5–0 First Division win at Tottenham Hotspur.

1988   England international left back Kenny Sansom joined Newcastle United. He won a then-Club-record 77 caps during his Highbury stint from 1980/81 to 1987/88.

2001   Giovanni van Bronckhorst was sent-off but Thierry Henry and Freddie Ljungberg scored in a 2–1 Premiership win at Liverpool.

24 December

1927 Joe Hulme, Charlie Buchan and Billy Blyth registered in Arsenal's 3–2 First Division win over Everton at Highbury.

1932 Jack Lambert scored five goals and Cliff Bastin notched a hat-trick as Arsenal swept to a crushing 9–2 First Division win over Sheffield United at Highbury.

1938 England Under-23 international John Barnwell was born in Newcastle. He netted 24 goals in 151 League games for Arsenal between 1956/57 and 1963/64.

1949 Reg Lewis, Alex Forbes, Peter Goring, Jimmy Logie and Ian McPherson all scored in Arsenal's 5–0 First Division win over Sunderland.

1958 Centre forward Len Julians arrived from Leyton Orient, with Stan Charlton and Tony Biggs moving in the opposite direction.

25 December

1886 It was resolved that Dial Square FC change its name to Royal Arsenal FC at a meeting at the Royal Oak public house in Woolwich.

1894 Paddy O'Brien netted a hat-trick as the Gunners charged to a 7–0 Second Division victory at home to Burslem Port Vale.

1934 Joe Hulme scored twice as title-chasing Arsenal gained a 5–3 First Division win over Preston North End at Highbury.

1951 Goals by Freddie Cox, Peter Goring, Reg Lewis and Jimmy Logie gave Arsenal a 4–1 First Division victory over Portsmouth at Highbury.

1952 Cliff Holton netted twice as Tom Whittaker's side secured a seasonably entertaining 6–4 First Division win over Bolton Wanderers at Burnden Park.

26 December

1929   Arsenal captain Tom Parker played his 172nd consecutive match, a current Club record, in the 2–1 defeat at home to Portsmouth.

1935   Bunny Bell scored nine goals as Tranmere Rovers gained a 13–4 win at home to Oldham Athletic, the record aggregate League score.

1963   Graham Leggat netted a hat-trick in three minutes during Fulham's 10–1 First Division win over Ipswich Town at Craven Cottage.

1983   Charlie Nicholas and Raphael Meade netted two goals apiece in the Gunners' 4–2 First Division triumph at Tottenham Hotspur.

2001   A 20-man fracas broke out at Highbury as Sol Campbell and Sylvain Wiltord scored in a 2–1 Premiership win at home to Chelsea.

27 December

1902   Tim Coleman bagged a hat-trick as Harry Bradshaw's team swept to a 5–1 Second Division victory at home to Burnley.

1972   Scotland midfielder George Graham was sold to Manchester United. He was reunited with his former Chelsea boss, ex-Gunner Tommy Docherty, at Old Trafford.

1977   Arsenal gained a 3–1 First Division win at West Bromwich Albion with goals by Alan Sunderland, Malcolm Macdonald and Liam Brady.

1984   Former Arsenal centre half Leslie Compton died aged 72 in his native Essex. He represented England at both football and cricket.

1993   Kevin Campbell's hat-trick plus a goal from Ian Wright earned the Gunners a 4–0 Premiership victory at Swindon Town.

28 December

1939   Scotland international Frank McLintock was born in Glasgow. He netted 26 goals in 314 League outings during a wondrous Arsenal career stretching from 1964/65 to 1972/73.

1963   Two goals by Johnny MacLeod plus others from Joe Baker and George Armstrong gave Arsenal a 4–1 First Division win at Birmingham City.

1965   George Eastham scored twice as Billy Wright's side gained a 5–2 First Division win over Sheffield Wednesday at Highbury.

1983   England Under-21 striker Lee Chapman was sold to Sunderland. A succession of injuries blighted his brief Highbury sojourn which resulted in six goals in 28 games for the Gunners.

1999   Strikes by Freddie Ljungberg and Thierry Henry gave the Gunners a 2–0 victory at home to leaders Leeds United.

29 December

1982   Yugoslav international midfielder Vladimir Petrovic arrived from Red Star Belgrade. He scored three times in 22 games for Arsenal during 1982/83.

1984   Two goals by Charlie Nicholas plus another from Brian Talbot secured Arsenal a 3–1 First Division win at Newcastle United.

1990   Substitute Andy Cole made his sole appearance for the Gunners in a 4–1 First Division victory over Sheffield United at Highbury.

1993   Arsenal gained a 3–0 Premiership win over Sheffield United with two goals by Kevin Campbell plus another from Ian Wright.

2001   Arsenal went top of the Premiership after Robert Pires and Ashley Cole scored in a 2–1 victory at home to Middlesbrough.

30 December

1922   Billy Blyth, Reg Boreham and Bobby Turnbull netted to give the Gunners a 3–0 First Division win at home to Stoke City.

1950   Peter Goring scored twice as Tom Whittaker's side gained a 2–0 First Division win over Sheffield Wednesday at Hillsborough.

1961   Scotland striker Charlie Nicholas, who played 20 times for his country, was born in Glasgow. He netted 54 goals in 184 outings for Arsenal between 1983/84 and 1987/88.

1978   Frank Stapleton, Graham Rix and Alan Sunderland netted to give Arsenal a 3–1 First Division win at home to Birmingham City.

2000   First-half goals by Patrick Vieira and Lee Dixon secured the Gunners a 2–2 Premiership draw against Sunderland at Highbury.

31 December

1898   Adam Haywood and Fergus Hunt grabbed hat-tricks as the Gunners gained a 6–2 Second Division victory at home to Luton Town.

1960   David Herd's hat-trick plus strikes by George Eastham and Jackie Henderson secured a 5–3 First Division triumph at Nottingham Forest.

1984   England international Steve Williams arrived from Southampton, while Brian McDermott left Highbury to join Oxford United.

1988   Alan Smith, David Rocastle and Perry Groves scored to give leaders Arsenal a 3–0 First Division victory at Aston Villa.

1994   John Jensen scored after 98 goalless games for Arsenal but was unable to prevent a 3–1 Premiership defeat by QPR at Highbury.

Notes

Notes